THE SERMON ON THE MOUNT

D0808606

The Sermon on the Mount
Daring to be different

Stuart Briscoe

OM PUBLISHING
Carlisle, U.K.

First published in the U.K. 1996
by arrangement with Harold Shaw Publishers,
Wheaton, Illinois, U.S.A.

OM Publishing is an imprint of Send the Light Ltd.,
P.O. Box 300, Carlisle, Cumbria CA3 0QS

02 01 00 99 98 97 96   7 6 5 4 3 2 1

A catalogue record for this book is available from the
British Library

ISBN 1-85078-198-2

Printed in the U.K. by Cox and Wyman Ltd., Reading

Contents

Study questions appear at the end of each chapter.

Introduction

When Jesus Christ arrived on the scene about two thousand years ago, it was easy to see that he was different. He had a delightful capacity for living among the men and women of his day, feeling their sorrows and enjoying their triumphs, yet avoiding their excesses and refuting their errors. He was thoroughly alive and alert, critical yet compassionate. Whether people were rich or poor appeared to concern him not at all. He seemed at ease in the midst of a group of belligerent theologians, coarse soldiers, or desperate sufferers. Composed and articulate, tough yet tender, he strode across a tiny corner of our world for a little over thirty years—and our world has never recovered from his visit.

The quality of his different life was matched only by the caliber of his shattering teaching. Living in a society uniquely rooted in tradition, he didn't hesitate to expose and explode cherished ideas where he felt such action was justified. He was death to duplicity; he hated hypocrisy. Yet he never stooped to being destructive and negative, and for one reason: He had come to reveal the truth of God through his life and his lips. This truth challenged error at every point; it exposed sin in every form; and where it challenged and exposed it invariably changed and recycled. Those who heard him and followed him as disciples became different as he was different.

Contemporary society needs change to survive. Its attention span is so short that it is bored in minutes. Its appetite for the thrilling and the different is so insatiable that it lurches from madcap scheme to ludicrous philosophy with alarming momentum. But with such change comes decay, and through the decay spreads disintegration. Change for the sake of change changes only the cover under which the decay continues. If only something different could be found that would not accelerate disintegration of life and society. Perhaps if Christ could come back, he could do something.

Idle thoughts? Not at all. For while he left for heaven and promised to return, he lives in our society through his body, the church. He is here to be as different as he always was, but you would not always know it. Why? For him to be seen in all his difference requires a church that is different from society—because it is composed of people who are different. And the difference of the church and the Christian is determined by the degree to which both live in obedience to his different teachings and reflect the dynamic of his indwelling presence.

In short, his disciples need to sit again at his feet and hear his Word. That will make a difference in them so radical that they will be different from their world, and the world will be changed because they passed through. I know of no better place to start than the Sermon on the Mount.

Now when he saw the crowds, he went up on a mountainside and sat down. His disciples came to him, and he began to teach them, saying . . .

Matthew 5:1-2

1

Christian Conduct

I believe this book is timely because there is so much public confusion as to what basic moral and ethical standards really are. This is true not only on the personal, individual level, but we are seeing moral and spiritual confusion on the national and international level as well. Many people are asking, How are we supposed to behave? Where do we find a moral code to live by? Where do we get the power and ability to live up to the moral and ethical standards that we have accepted?

I believe the Lord Jesus has anticipated our questions and has already given us the answers—in his discourse known as the Sermon on the Mount. In it he expressed principles—moral, ethical, and social—that come from his eternal mind and have to do with men and women of all ages. These principles are tremendously relevant to people who are in the kingdom. But just one word of warning here: Jesus' teachings given in the Sermon on the Mount were given to his disciples. They were not broadcast generally.

One problem we have is that we try to get a fallen society to behave as if it were made up of Christians, and that's something we will never do. Our big problem is not getting a fallen society to behave like Christians. The big problem is to get Christians to stop behaving like fallen society! If only we could get Christians to act like Christians, we would discover that the principles enunciated here produce a totally different moral, ethical, and social standard, making Christian behavior distinctive and unlike that of the rest of the world. In the Sermon on the Mount, Jesus is telling his disciples, "Now look. If you're really going to be my men and my women, you're going to be bucking the rest of society in just about every conceivable area."

But tragically, Christians have lost their distinctiveness. Because they have, and because they have failed to be what God intends them to be in any society, society as a whole has lost the Christian voice. As a result, society has lost its salt, its guiding light. It has lost its "city set on a hill," the example that Jesus said Christians were to be. Perhaps the way to national revival is not to impose upon a lost society principles they will never be able to accept. Rather, the way to national revival is to get Christians once again to begin to adhere to the social, moral, and ethical standards set forth in the Sermon on the Mount—the norm for Christian experience in the midst of a lost society. Perhaps then once again we will begin to produce Christians who buck the stream, Christians who are a thorn in the flesh to a system that is godless. Once again Christians will become what they were intended to be—the salt of the earth, the city set on a hill, the light of the world. And maybe then, once again, society will begin to see the effectiveness of the ministry of Jesus Christ.

Why Do We Do What We Do?

There are three areas involved in the behavior mechanism of a normal human being. We all have motivational forces, and superimposed upon our motivational forces are certain moral factors. Usually these motivational and moral factors are, to a large extent, in opposition to each other. At this point a third factor comes into play: the mechanism for choice. This choice mechanism is the referee. It keeps the other two opposing factors at arm's length and makes them complementary rather than competitive.

Motivational forces

Motivational forces have to do with the self. Unfortunately, in evangelical Christianity the term *self* usually has a bad connotation. But self is not necessarily bad. For example, Jesus tells us that we are to love our neighbor as ourselves (Matt. 19:19), so obviously self-love is a biblical concept. In God's eyes his children are important—they have worth. There is a divine dimension in each of us. As we begin to see this eternal evaluation of the human being, we discover certain elements that God has put into us, basic natural motivational forces. Three of these are self-preservation, self-gratification, and self-glorification. Almost automatically we react negatively to these terms—they're all bad; anyone interested in self-preservation, self-gratification, or self-glorification is sinful. Not necessarily. They are part of the built-in motivational mechanism that is necessary to make us behave as human beings.

For instance, when a baby begins to crawl around and touches something hot, what happens? The very first time a baby is introduced to fire, he learns something. He learns that fire burns. What is built into a baby's mind as a result of that little burned hand? He learns a certain fear of fire. This is what we call *self-preservation.*

There is a second motivational force—*self-gratification.* When a little baby is born, what does he or she do quite soon? The baby demonstrates an insatiable desire for food. This is a form of self-gratification known as hunger. This desire for self-gratification is tremendously important. If the baby didn't have it, he'd starve. There would be no way the baby could survive without this inborn motivation. If we didn't have certain self-preservation motivational factors, we would not survive in a basically hostile world. These are survival mechanisms. They're all an inherent part of our behavior.

The third motivational force is *self-glorification.* This, too, is evidenced quite early in life. A baby soon learns he can get attention by opening his mouth wide and yelling at the top of his voice. In fact, he will probably pull every trick in the book to make absolutely certain he gets all the attention possible! And that's perfectly natural. Babies need this instinct to survive.

Obviously, all these basic motivational forces in human behavior produce individual drives. They produce a person who's going to look out for number one. *I've* got to survive. *I've* got to be kept out of danger. *I* must have love. And so it goes. Without these drives mankind wouldn't and couldn't survive.

Moral factors

It's also perfectly obvious where those demands can lead us. That's why God has also equipped us not only with motivational forces, but also with moral factors. The moral factors built into human beings may also be classified under three headings. First of all, the *conscience* is a built-in factor. In his Epistle to the Romans, Paul points out that there are certain concepts common to all human beings (Rom. 1:18ff.). There is a law written in people's hearts. Many people consider this sensitivity to God's law to be the conscience. Every human being has a certain conscience.

As a baby begins to grow, he finds himself in conflict with certain basic egocentric drives. Because he is a member of a civilized society, some of these basic drives cannot be exercised to the full. The growing person begins to discover he has to live not only in terms of himself, but in terms of other people as well. Through these overall controlling forces, conscience begins to work. And conscience begins to flash a warning light whenever the young person violates the rights of others in his drive to satisfy his own desires. Basic motivational drives are being tempered by basic moral factors, and the still small voice of conscience is beginning to speak.

In addition to the effect of moral factors upon the conscience, *community thinking* also comes into play. Those of us who travel widely notice how community thinking varies from place to place. As you wander around the world and see the differences in people's behavior patterns, you begin to understand that the differences in behavior patterns are developed through variations in community thinking. Consider how community thinking varies from the inner city to suburbia. It differs even more markedly between countries, and between geographic areas like the Middle East and the Far East. Wherever you go you will find that communities think in totally different ways. We in the United States consider ourselves highly civilized, more so than most other parts of the world. But are we?

I was in South America not long ago and spent some time with one of the primitive tribes. This tribe had an interesting custom, too interesting for me to share in complete detail! Let me just give you a broad overview. In that tribe when a girl arrived at the age of puberty, she climbed a tree. Since the area was rather barren, there weren't many trees, so she was immediately noticeable! In case she wasn't noticed, she sang. I don't know the exact words of the song, but the message was basically, "I'm available." This was what she sang from the top of her tree.

Naturally, the men of the tribe responded positively to her message, and they began to appear from all points of the compass. The law of the tribe was simple: she belonged to the first guy to pull her down out of the tree! Again, quite naturally, children were born of the resulting union. The tribal law stipulated that when children were born as a result of this alliance, it was incumbent on the parents to establish a home for the child—or the infant must be killed. The couple could go through this over and over again as children were born out of this "alliance" (which was perfectly legitimate by community standards).

Then one day the couple could decide they wanted to be regarded as married. They could announce their decision by keeping a child. The first child kept was evidence that now they were married. At that point stringent community regulations came into effect. Now certain rules against adultery prevailed. If any married person committed adultery in that tribe, then the chief would slash open the back of his neck with the "adulterer's knife" kept specifically for that purpose. This is an example of the community thinking of a primitive Indian tribe.

Notice the similarities between that tribe and so-called civilization today. Plenty of our young ladies today go around announcing, "I'm available," once they have reached the age of puberty or slightly older. They don't climb trees, they just dress that way. They don't sing songs, they just announce it in other ways. The message is unmistakable to any male with his eyes open. The message is loud and clear: "I am available." We're as civilized as that primitive tribe in the South American jungle. And we're no different when it comes to unwanted children. Unwanted offspring from this alliance are also done away with. Our parents don't bury the babies alive as the Indian tribe does. They abort them. Our principle of operation in so-called civilization is at least as bad as the principle of operation in the primitive society. The difference is this: They have an "adulterer's knife" and we don't. We condone adultery. I have said all this to make a point. We need to be very careful when we evaluate other community standards of behavior. In many instances, our so-called civilization is drastically uncivilized in comparison with even the most primitive tribes.

Our moral factors are also built as a result of convictions that are introduced. This is where parents come in. God gave us children to raise. One of the major breakdowns in society today is right at this point: the total failure of the home to introduce valid convictions, which in turn produce moral factors to control motivational forces.

The mechanism of choice

The third element involved in the dynamics of human behavior is the mechanism of choice. What happens when the drives for self-gratification, self-glorification, or self-preservation are such that a person's moral principles are in total opposition? A conflict arises, and the outcome of that conflict is determined by the mechanism of choice given to every human being by God. The mechanism of choice is the ability to discern a valid motivational force and a valid moral factor. The mechanism of choice gives me the ability to discriminate and discern between what is a valid moral principle and what is a totally amoral principle. I then begin to make decisions. Every decision is a product of discernment and discrimination. It isn't really surprising to me that our human behavior in today's world has gone berserk. Often we human beings haven't even tried to understand what really is involved in the dynamics of human behavior.

Why Is It So Difficult to Be Different?

When our motivational forces of self-preservation, self-gratification, and self-glorification are unrestrained, terrible difficulties in human behavior emerge. Think of the businessman plagued by this problem of self-preservation. He is primarily interested in preserving his position. Morality does not matter. The only thing that matters to him is his own survival and success—at any price. This is one of the main causes of our problems in American and Western European society today. In many cases, we have a business ethic that is nothing more than unrestrained self-preservation. In the business world, this kind of attitude in management generates the same reaction in employees. They band together to form a union, and they elect a fiery negotiator to represent them. What is his main interest? Self-preservation. In the resulting battle, industry begins to come apart at the seams. Why? Because of unrestrained motivational forces—people convinced that self-preservation is all that matters.

Now let's add the urge toward self-gratification. If a person is mainly concerned with gratifying himself, then he is not really going to be careful about how he gets that gratification. The important thing is that it "pleases me." In our Western civilization, we are producing people who have been taught that anything is legitimate if it makes "me" happy. Morality and motivation do not matter as long as I am satisfied.

This is where the church of Jesus Christ is supposed to speak out loud and clear. Christians are to warn our world: "Look, one of our major problems is this: Our lax moral standards are allowing chaos to enter and operate in our society. That's why humanity is where it is." History reveals that the church sometimes goes overboard and overreacts against weak moral standards. Often in reaction the church produces too stringent a moral standard, confusing and alienating the world around it. So it is possible to get into difficulties either way, whether the motivational forces are unrestrained or the moral factors are unsatisfactory.

I don't believe our major problem in society is either of these two; our major problem is simple mechanical breakdown. The three dynamics (motivational, moral, and mechanical) all have the same potential failure. Obviously, the moral can go wrong. So, too, can the motivational. But the mechanism of choice is the area usually overlooked today. And it is here that we need to be fully alert and alive. In Romans 7 Paul writes about the sort of confusion that exists in a person's life if his motivational and moral forces are battling and he is incapable of making a choice through the mechanism God has given him. Paul says, "For what I do is not the good I want to do; no, the evil I do not want to do—this I keep on doing" (Rom. 7:19). A person in this bind wants to do a certain thing, but knows it is wrong. Here we see the motivational battling with the moral. This is humanity's major problem: an impasse between unrestrained motivational forces and uneducated moral factors which is not adequately resolved because we are incapable of making the right decisions.

Ungodly people do not have the spiritual experience necessary to equip them to discern, discriminate, and decide correctly. This is where the distinctiveness of Christian behavior comes in. True Christianity demands a standard of behavior above and beyond that which society has decided is normal. As we look further into the Sermon on the Mount, you will begin to see what I mean.

How Is Christian Behavior Different?

Let me point out four distinctives of Christian behavior that we find in this introduction to the Sermon on the Mount. First of all, there's the matter of *morality*. If there's going to be a distinctive Christian behavior, there is going to be a distinctive *Christian* morality. Underline this thought. Many different moral systems are abroad today. You can divide them into two main groups. One school of thought is based on human speculation, the result of man, sitting down here, scratching his head and trying to figure out which way to go. The other school of thought is based on divine revelation. God, speaking from heaven, is saying, "This is the way; walk in it." The two systems are in total conflict. One section of society is saying, "Where on earth are we going?" The result is speculative philosophy—that produces speculative morality—that produces speculative disaster. At the same time God is saying, "This is the way; walk in it." When Jesus sat on the mountaintop, gathering his disciples around him, he was saying, "Fellows, listen to me. Don't listen to the world around you. Simply listen to me. I am going to reveal to you a system of morality that is workable."

Morality that works comes from mountaintop revelation, not human speculation. As Christians, our norm for behavior must come from God. Any Christian who tries to operate on society's behavior patterns had better recheck his or her Christianity. Our morality must come from above. Our ethics, our morals, our behavior patterns are to be found in the Word of God.

Secondly, it's a matter of *mentality,* a matter of learning at Jesus' feet. This is what the disciples did. Matthew sets the scene: "Now when he saw the crowds, he went up on a mountainside and sat down. His disciples came to him, and he began to teach them" (5:1-2). Behavior comes from mentality, and mentality is set alight by the teachings of Jesus Christ. The eternal principles he enunciated are the bases of distinctive Christian behavior. We have a mentality that comes from above, from Jesus Christ himself. We do not learn from experimenting along with the rest of the world, but from the teaching that comes from the Lord of glory.

The third distinctive is a matter of *mastery.* We Christians are not supposed to be on an ego trip. We are to be disciples. Jesus said, "Discipleship is simply this. You take up your cross and follow me daily. If you live your own life, you'll lose it. But if you lose your life in mine, you'll find it." That is the attitude of surrender that is the total antithesis of the ego trip.

I'm afraid much that passes for Christianity today is nothing more than glorified human speculation. It is nothing more or less than a glorified evangelical ego trip. This is our problem. We need a new morality, a new mentality, a new mastery. This is the basis of distinctive Christian behavior.

And finally, it's a matter of *minority*. I get a great kick out of the Lord Jesus seeing the multitudes and calling twelve men to one side. He said, "Fellows, see that multitude? Let's hit the multitude." How is he going to do it? By getting a nucleus, a minority. He is going to work with the minority to change the majority. I may be rather cynical, but I think the multitude is very often wrong. This may run contrary to your political thinking, but I believe it. What a delightful thing it is to be a Christian, knowing you're always going to be in the minority. And you know, it takes a certain kind of minority thinking to produce distinctive Christianity. That's what we're after.

MAKING IT PRACTICAL

1. Why are we as Christians often ineffective and inaccurate in representing Christ to the world?

2. What part does our "mechanism of choice" play in the tension between our natural tendencies and what we know is right?

3. What are some specific ways we see motivating factors such as self-preservation, self-gratification, and self-glorification running amok in our society today?

4. How has this preoccupation with "self" affected many of us as Christians?

5. How can Christians make a difference in such a self-oriented society?

Blessed are the poor in spirit,
   for theirs is the kingdom of heaven.
Blessed are those who mourn,
   for they will be comforted.
Blessed are the meek,
   for they will inherit the earth.
Matthew 5:3-5

2

Christian Happiness

A divine minority against a secular majority. This is the way I would describe what it means to be a distinctive, dynamic, supernormal Christian in our modern-day society.

As Jesus begins to teach his disciples in the Sermon on the Mount, what is the very first word he utters? It is the word *blessed*. He doesn't just say it once; he repeats it a total of eight times. I think he meant for us to take particular notice of it! The word *blessed* is a rather lovely word often used by us without our really understanding what it means. In the Greek it is *makarios*. The Greek people thought their gods had it made, and they used the word to describe this unbelievable state of well-being in which the gods lived. This is the word used by the Lord in the New Testament as he begins to describe the life he has come to give to his people— a life of blessedness.

Makarios living is what Jesus has in mind for his people. He wants us to live in a state of contentment, a state of fulfillment. We are to live in a state of happiness, a state of joy. As I look around me in the church, I think in some instances we have lost this message. The church has become involved in many areas of ministry, but I'm afraid we've forgotten that the Lord Jesus came to earth to instill unbelievable blessedness, *makarios,* in people's lives.

This should not surprise us. When Paul wrote to Timothy, he called God "the blessed God" (1 Tim. 1:11). This concept of God is not difficult to grasp. We have no difficulty picturing him as contented, fulfilled, and complete. But do we ever think of God as being happy? God is in essence happy, joyful. He is in essence *makarios.* It would be rather strange if this blessed God did not want to produce blessed people. A thoroughly happy God must want to make people happy. If only we Christians could begin to get back to the idea that our Lord came into this world, not to put people into evangelical straitjackets, not to put them under rigid systems that squeeze the joy out of their existence, but to fill them full so they would go around the world and bring a message of *makarios.*

Of course, there are hindrances to blessing, to happiness, to contentment and fulfillment. Two words describe these hindrances: selfishness and sinfulness. Therefore, if a happy God is going to bring happy people to himself, do you know what he must do? He has to pinpoint the hindrances and eradicate them. There never was a thoroughly selfish man who was a truly happy man. A sinful man just cannot enjoy *makarios* living. Sin and selfishness stand in the way of our blessedness. Many Christians have the idea that sharing the gospel of Jesus Christ is telling sinners that they need to be convicted of their sin, telling selfish people to be unselfish. That isn't the gospel. That is simply pinpointing the hindrances between us and what God has in mind for us. We cannot combine blessedness with sinfulness and selfishness. If we want blessedness, which is God's norm for society, sinfulness and selfishness have to go. This is what Jesus is saying with his repetition of the word *blessed.*

In England a number of years ago we did a survey. We asked hundreds of young people, "What is your main ambition?" Most of them answered, "To be happy." They wanted happiness more than anything else. Some said they wanted to be married, that they expected to find happiness in that state. Most were not looking for money or fame. Having these things does not guarantee happiness.

The great quest of the human soul, wherever you go throughout this wide world of ours, is basically, "How can I find *makarios?*" I'm excited and thrilled because as a Christian I have the answer to that basic life question. I represent a blessed God who wants men and women to have true happiness. As we begin to look at the Beatitudes in this chapter, we're going to discover what God has in mind for us. We're going to look in depth at just three of them, and we will see as we do that happiness is the product of character, and happiness is the promise of Christ.

Most people think that happiness is to be found in things. Actually, true happiness is to be found only in a right relationship with the God who alone gives reason and content to living. When we know him, he brings joy through the things he has graciously given. But real happiness is not rooted in material things. It is independent of them. Possession of things is mere selfishness. It is a pseudohappiness rooted in selfishness. God is the blessed God. From him comes blessedness. Here in the Sermon on the Mount Jesus goes on to point out that the happiness he's talking about is not related to the temporal or the secular, the tangible or the material. Basically a spiritual experience, it is above these things.

Happiness Is a Product of Character

The first thing Jesus points out is that happiness is a product of a certain kind of character. Certain phrases in verses 3-5 bear this out: "Blessed are the poor in spirit, . . . those who mourn," and "the meek." These three statements are a paradox to the modern mind. They fly right in the face of general opinion. "Blessed are the poor in spirit? Baloney!" says the secular man. "You have to get out there and do your own thing. You have to hack out your own little niche in the wilderness of the world." That's a rather simplified translation of society's philosophy.

With all due respect, I would label that philosophy "Baloney." The United States of America is filled with people who have lived by this erroneous philosophy, and they've hacked out their piece of the continent. They can stand on it with their feet firmly planted and their hands on their hips—and still they're miserable. Happiness does not come from centering one's life around oneself. No, blessedness comes only to the poor in spirit.

You ask, "How can a person who's poor in spirit ever know happiness? If he's poverty-stricken in spirit, he's going to be unhappy because he's poor." Paradoxically enough, that isn't the way it works.

Look at it from God's perspective. When we recognize what we are, then we are ready to look at God realistically. When we know our need, then we're interested in what God gives. And what God gives is blessedness in the midst of what we are. Only a certain kind of character will admit that kind of need.

Happiness is being realistic

What kind of character is "poor in spirit"? Such a person is thoroughly realistic about his or her situation in two particular areas: spiritual inability and spiritual inadequacy. This person comes before God and says, "God, you're the great God, and I'm only a little piece of your creation. I have my own little world, and it's crumbling. I did my own thing, and it is not satisfying. I sought happiness everywhere people said it could be found, and I didn't find it. I have climbed to the end of the rainbow, and there was no pot of gold. Now what?"

The Lord comes back to this person and says, "I'll tell you what we'll do. Let's backtrack a bit, and let's look at you." Then the Lord points out that outside of Christ we are poverty-stricken in spirit, and that unless and until this is rectified, we can never find fulfillment.

Realistic about our spiritual inability. One of our main problems is that we do not recognize our true spiritual condition. This is what makes happiness so elusive. We are utterly poverty-stricken spiritually because we're completely devoid of spiritual ability. The spiritual poverty of human beings is beautifully described by Jesus in the word *cannot.* "Jesus said . . . , 'verily, verily, I say unto thee,

Except a man be born again he *cannot* see the kingdom of God' " (John 3:3, KJV, italics mine).

We are so spiritually inadequate and incapable that the Bible has to tell us what we can't do. Until we face up to our need, we'll never be interested in what God can do in our lives. Our interest will be in what we can do ourselves. And until we allow God to do in our lives what we cannot do for ourselves, we will never know *makarios*. Our root problem is simply refusing to admit, "I am spiritually incapable. I simply cannot enter the kingdom of heaven on my own."

This admission of weakness is one of the hardest things to do. When we have bought the philosophy that we can do anything if we put our mind to it, we find it impossible to say, "I can't." But let's face it. There's one thing we cannot do. We cannot enter the kingdom of heaven. That's a hard statement, but it's the truth. If we would only admit how poverty-stricken we are, then we might be interested in the blessedness that comes to poverty-stricken people who say, "Here I am, God. I can't enter the kingdom of heaven. Oh, God, do something for me." And he does. What does he do? *Makarios*.

Let's see what Jesus says to some religious leaders in another place. "You will look for me, but you will not find me; and where I am, you *cannot come*" (John 7:34, italics mine). We say, "I can go any place I want. I can do anything I want to do. I can be anything I want to be. And if I go where I want to go, and be where I want to be, and do what I want to do, I'll be happy." Sounds great, but there's only one problem. There are some things we can't do, and there are some places we can't go, because of our spiritual inability and inadequacy. Let me give some scriptural examples of what I mean:

The realistic character is the one who says, "I am poor in spirit. There's so much I can't do." In John 15:4 Jesus said, "Remain in me, and I will remain in you. No branch can bear fruit by itself; it must remain in the vine. Neither can you bear fruit unless you remain in me." We say, "I can produce if I want to. I could produce. I will produce." But God says, "No, you won't." We simply cannot.

No way! There is no hope for us, says the Lord Jesus. We cannot produce what God expects a human being to produce apart from a relationship with Jesus Christ, any more than a branch can produce fruit when it has been severed from the tree. It isn't that the branch won't produce fruit. It is simply that the branch *cannot* produce fruit.

Paul tells us the same thing: "Those controlled by the sinful nature *cannot* please God" (Rom. 8:8, italics added). We say, "I'll please God when I want to. I don't want to right now, but I will when I'm ready. When I'm really happy. When I've got it made. When I've done what I want to, gone where I want to go, then I'll give God a chance, and I'll make God happy." God says, "No, you won't." We don't have what it takes in ourselves apart from God's grace. He must pour into us *makarios* before we can please him.

We're never going to be interested in what God can pour into us until we realize how empty and incapable we really are. The divine principle, the controversial, paradoxical principle of happiness is totally the opposite of what the world says. The world says, "Get up there; build yourself up there; be what you're going to be, and you'll be happy." God says, "Humble yourself. Admit what you are. Face the poverty of your own spiritual experience, and then I'll pour in *makarios*. Blessed are those who are realistic enough in character to admit their own spiritual inability."

Realistic about our spiritual inadequacy. To be poor in spirit also means to be realistic about our own spiritual *inadequacy*. Three Bible characters come to mind here: Jacob, Isaiah, and Gideon. They all had something in common. God wanted to bless them, to fill them, to use them. But he couldn't bless any of them, or fill them, or use them—until something very beautiful happened to each of them. They had to face their poverty of spirit. They not only had to admit their own spiritual inability, but also their own spiritual inadequacy.

What happened to Jacob? He fought God all night until God dislocated his hip, putting him flat on his back. Then he said, "Okay, God. I quit. I can't buck your system. I can't win. I can't be what I'm supposed to be without allowing you to be the God you intend to be. All right, I surrender." The Bible says, "Then he [God] blessed him there" (Gen. 32:29). *Makarios.* The hardest thing for a person to do is to admit poverty of spirit, but it's the only path to real happiness.

God was going to do fantastic things with Isaiah. He wanted him to be a beautiful prophet of the Old Testament, but something was in the way. Isaiah was all upset because the king had died. That's all he could think about—his loss. What did God do? God graciously gave Isaiah a vision of himself high and exalted. The train of God's robe filled the temple. Isaiah saw the majestic heavenly temple and the throne. He saw the majestic, heavenly God. What did Isaiah say? "Woe to me! . . . I am ruined! For I am a man of unclean lips, . . . and my eyes have seen the King, the LORD Almighty" (Isa. 6:5). In effect God was saying, "Isaiah, you're right. Woe is you. You are a man of unclean lips. You have seen the Lord. You're right. You don't have what it takes. Blessed are the poor in spirit." *Makarios.* And God blessed Isaiah there.

God was going to do something with Gideon, who was having trouble with his harvest. When it was all ready, his enemies would come at night and steal it. So Gideon decided to get ahead of them and harvest it before it was ripe. He hid behind the walls of his winepress to do his threshing. And what did God do? With a delightful touch of humor, God's angel says, "The LORD is with you, mighty warrior" (Judg. 6:12). Mighty warrior? Right away Gideon began to make excuses. He wasn't the man for the job of conquering the enemy. But God said, "Go in the strength you have and save Israel" (Judg. 6:14). What kind of a man was Gideon? He was totally aware of his own spiritual inadequacy until God touched him and said, "Listen, mighty warrior. I'm with you. This is your strength." *Makarios.* Now he could go out and *be* the mighty warrior. Gideon finds contentment and fulfillment. If we were to ask him, "Gideon, what is happiness?" he would reply, "Happiness is just being realistic about yourself. It is admitting how poor in spirit you are and saying, 'Oh, God, what I need is you.'"

Happiness is being repentant

In Matthew 5 the Lord Jesus not only says, "Blessed are the poor in spirit." He goes on to say, "Blessed are those who mourn." It's part of the same package. We cannot be realistic about our own spiritual inability and our own spiritual inadequacy and leave it there. When we realize our own poverty of spirit, we begin to understand the necessity for repentance. There is no happiness for the person who sees what is wrong with himself or herself and does nothing about it. "Blessed are those who mourn" does not refer only to people who sit at a graveside. It refers to much more. Repentance comes deep in the soul when we realize all God has in mind for us and how little of it we have appropriated. When we begin to understand what God wants to do with, for, in, and through us, and we look at what has not been achieved, our heart breaks. There is no *makarios* for the unrepentant. There is no fulfillment for those who reject the truth about themselves. We must come in brokenness, contrition, and confession before God.

Read Psalm 51 to see how David did it. He not only saw how utterly poverty-stricken he was, but he was also repentant, broken-hearted before God. So he confessed his sin.

Look at Job. Job had so much of everything, he didn't know what to do with it. Butter was scarce where he lived. Yet he had so much butter he washed his front doorstep with it (Job 29:6, KJV). That seems rather a strange custom—must have made the steps terribly slippery! But that's Job. He was the greatest, but he wasn't happy until he reached the point of Job 42:6, "I despise myself and repent in dust and ashes." Apparently it took forty-one chapters to bring Job to that point of repentance. And God says, "Amen. Job's made it. Blessed are the poor in spirit. Blessed are those who mourn. You've come to the point of realism. You've come to the point of repentance." And God gave Job an oversized dose of *makarios*. Job was now happiness personified.

Happiness is the product of a character that is realistic and repentant before God. There is no *makarios* for the unrealistic and the unrepentant. Such people are fighting a losing battle and running a losing race.

Happiness is being responsive

The third beatitude is "Blessed are the meek." People say if you're going to be happy, you must go out into the big, hard, materialistic world and give it all you have. The world's idea of meekness is being a doormat, having spaghetti for a backbone.

But meekness isn't synonymous with weakness! The word literally means "yieldedness." It is the natural product of a realistic character that is poor in spirit and repentant character that mourns because of its poverty. A realistic, repentant character knows the only alternative is responsive yielding to the blessed God. Meekness isn't weakness. It's the opposite. It takes a certain moral strength to admit how desperately we need God and yield unreservedly to him. Why are there so many unhappy people in the world? Because they will not admit how poverty-stricken they are. They will not mourn for their sin, nor will they yield to God. That's why they are unhappy.

Jesus says, on the other hand, "Don't listen to all this stuff the world gives you. What I'm telling you is controversial—it's paradoxical. It runs counter to everything the world will tell you. But it's the truth. Will you admit your own inability, you own inadequacy? Will you mourn for your sin? Will you face your own situation and confess your sin? And then will you be responsive?"

Happiness is the product of character that is realistic, repentant, and responsive. Jesus said, "Blessed are the poor in spirit. . . . Blessed are those who mourn. . . . Blessed are the meek." He could have approached it from the opposite point of view: "Unblessed are the arrogant in spirit and self-sufficient. Singularly unblessed are those unrepentant, hard-necked, unyielding, uncommitted, unresponsive people. The unfulfilled are discontent and unhappy, completely devoid of joy." The blessed God says, "If only they knew what I have in store for them. If only they'd do it my way." Happiness is the product of character.

Happiness Is the Promise of Christ

Notice three things here concerning the promises Christ gives. First is the *authority* of his statements. The Lord Jesus didn't just sit there apologetically on the Mount and say, "Now, fellows, listen. Blessed are the poor in spirit, I think. Blessed are those who mourn, so I understand. Blessed are the meek, so I've been told. You see, fellows, I don't know how it works, but I think the poor in spirit are blessed because I think God might give them a little piece of the kingdom. I'm not sure, but I think so. And I think those who mourn are blessed because I think God will comfort them. You know, he's like that." Jesus just did not talk that way.

Notice the calm certainty of his statements: "Blessed are the poor in spirit, for *theirs is* the kingdom of heaven. Blessed are those who mourn, for they *will* be comforted. Blessed are the meek, for they *will* inherit the earth." He declared it unequivocally. I use the repetitive to emphasize this point: Blessing is what God has for his people. The authority of Jesus is rooted in the authoritative God who says, "This is the way it is." To find happiness we merely accept.

Secondly, I must understand the *availability* of his blessings. What is the blessing available for the poor in spirit? The kingdom of heaven. What is the blessing for those who mourn? Comfort. For those who are meek? They will inherit the earth.

What is God saying here? He is saying that if a person will admit total inadequacy and inability in the spiritual realm, if he or she will confess it, repent of it, and yield to God, God will give that person the kingdom. He or she will have unbelievable riches in exchange for unbearable poverty.

Then Jesus added: "Anyone who will repent, and come in brokenness and contrition before me, will be comforted and forgiven." The Greek word translated "comforted" here is closely related to the name given the Holy Spirit—the Comforter. It doesn't mean just someone coming along and patting you on the head, mopping your fevered brow. It means "one called alongside to help and to impart strength." This is entering the kingdom and enjoying its riches, appropriating the Comforter and knowing his strength.

Jesus also says, "Blessed are the meek, for they will inherit the earth." Perhaps a better translation is "They will inherit the land." Remember how the Israelites went into the new land and possessed it? After routing their enemies, they set their feet firmly on what God had given them and thoroughly enjoyed it. Oh, blessed are the meek. They're going to rout their enemies; they're going to stand firm in all that God has formed for them; they're going to possess their possessions.

Let's look one final time at the word *makarios*. The *makarios* is all the riches of the kingdom imparted to poverty-stricken people. It is all the strength of the Comforter given to broken people. It is nothing less than the possession of all our possessions and the routing of all our enemies. All we have to do is come in yieldedness to God. Where then does the happiness come from? It comes through the acceptance of what Jesus offers. Outside of Christ, a person must say, "I am singularly unblessed. Now I know why. I accept the authority of your statements. I believe in the availability of your blessings, and I accept all that you have in mind for me. I come humbly, contritely, broken in spirit. I come to you in faith." When a person can say this, he or she is on the way to blessing, fulfillment, contentment, and happiness. This shouldn't surprise us, because we have a blessed God! Let's live *makariosly.*

MAKING IT PRACTICAL

1. What does Jesus mean by the word translated "blessed"? What does this word really mean?

2. What are some of the things that effectively keep people from being blessed, happy, content, and fulfilled?

3. What makes it so difficult for people, especially in our society, to admit that there are things we simply cannot do without God's help?

4. What does it mean to you to be realistic about your spiritual condition? Where are you right now in these stages of realism, repentance, and responsiveness?

Blessed are those who hunger and thirst for righteousness,
   for they will be filled.
Blessed are the merciful,
   for they will be shown mercy.
Blessed are the pure in heart,
   for they will see God.

Matthew 5:6-8

3

And More Happiness

In this chapter we are continuing to look at happiness as a product of character. There are three aspects of the matter I'd like you to note: ambition, attitude, and action. In Matthew 5:6 Jesus talks about those who "hunger and thirst for righteousness." Hungering and thirsting is a rather descriptive term for *ambition*. God requires a certain kind of character in those who would follow him. They are to be ambitious, but theirs is to be an ambition based on that which is right. This commitment to the right is the basis of the blessing of God in my life. The full flow of his blessing comes from his righteousness lived out in me.

The next Beatitude (Matt. 5:7) calls for a certain *attitude* in the child of God: "Blessed are the merciful, for they will be shown mercy." The word for "merciful" might better be translated "kind." If my ambition is based on that which is right and my attitude on that which is kind, then I will begin to see God producing in me the full flow of his blessing.

If God's intention were simply to take Christians to heaven, he would lead them to a decision and then whisk them off. But that is not his plan. His intention is to make Christians and leave them on earth that they might be a channel for change in society. The people who create change are those who know the blessing of God, who have their attitudes right.

The third Beatitude calls for a certain *action,* action based on truth. Jesus says, "Blessed are the pure in heart, for they will see God" (Matt. 5:8). When you read the word *pure* in this context in Scripture, it means singleness of mind and purpose. Is our world today characterized by action? Definitely yes. But are the actions seen in our world today absolutely based on integrity, sincerity, and truthfulness? Emphatically no. That is the degree to which our society needs the church of Jesus Christ. The beautiful thing about being a Christian and a member of the church of Jesus Christ is this: We are called to be totally different and distinctive. As we are, the blessing of God comes upon our lives.

One of the mistakes many Christians make today is this: They want to be just like the world and also blessed of God. This is impossible. We can be just like the society around us, with ambition like theirs, an attitude like theirs, and involvement in activities like theirs—but forget the *makarios* in that case. On the other hand, we can major on the *makarios.* We can say, "God, nothing really matters to me more than your blessing upon my life." In that case, our activities are going to change from those of the world around us. We're going to be God's men and women in society, receiving his blessing. That is the promise of Christ.

Ambition

Ambition is normal. A person without ambition, lacking motivation, has a problem (besides being lazy!). Such a person needs to discover he has worth. A human being can never be worthless, for he is divinely created. God created him to fulfill a certain function. His overriding ambition, at least, ought to be to find out why God made him.

It is proper to have ambition—it is an integral part of our personhood. It is an integral part of being what God intended human beings to be. But that ambition may be perverted. Examples from Scripture show us that perversion of ambition is quite possible.

Look with me at Lucifer, son of the morning, one of God's most glorious creations, a masterpiece. He was supremely beautiful and absolutely magnificent. What was his driving ambition? Isaiah records it for us: "You said in your heart, 'I will ascend to heaven; I will raise my throne above the stars of God; I will sit enthroned on the mount of assembly. . . . I will ascend above the tops of the clouds; I will make myself like the Most High' " (Isa. 14:13-14).

The driving ambition of Lucifer's soul was to be like God! He was power-hungry. Anyone who is hungry for power for its own sake is a victim of perverted ambition. But you will find these power-hungry people in the big arena of national politics, or in the small arena of the local church. You will find them everywhere—bullies in the school, teachers behind the desks. In the business world this craze for power runs rampant.

This is a perversion of ambition which God totally rejects. When Lucifer made his grab for power, how did God react? Isaiah gives us his reply to Lucifer's boast: "But you are brought down" (14:15).

In the parable of the rich fool recorded in Luke 12, Jesus spoke of a certain rich man who had done well in business. One day he thought to himself, *What shall I do? I have no place to store my crops?* (12:17). So he decided to pull down his old barns and build larger ones. That sounds like good business practice. What's wrong with that ambition? Nothing at all. If God has given a businessman intelligence and ability, then God is going to bless him. He is going to say, "Go right ahead, friend, because every penny you make is mine. The more you make for me the more pleased I'll be."

Make no mistake about it. God is going to give some people the ability to gain wealth, and others will not have as much of this ability. This is what creates the difficulty. Wealth always brings problems along with it. Those who have money have problems knowing what to do with it. And those who do not have money encounter problems trying to get it.

What did the man in the parable do? He tore down his old barns and built larger ones, saying to his soul in the process, "You have plenty of good things laid up for many years. Take life easy; eat, drink and be merry" (Luke 12:19). His goal was to make as big a pile as possible so he could retire and enjoy himself. His problem was not power-hunger—it was pleasure-hunger. Hungering and thirsting after fun, he was absolutely eaten up with the desire to have a good time. It's very interesting to note God's commentary on this kind of ambition. God used one word to describe him: "Fool!" (Luke 12:20). Need I say more? God has a succinct way of expressing himself, doesn't he? When a man's ambition is perverted to power-hunger, God brings him down. And when a man's ambition is simply devoted to pleasure-seeking, God calls him a fool and brings him down.

Daniel tells us about another example of perverted ambition. Nebuchadnezzar was doing pretty well, but he was hungry for more fame. He loved the adulation of the crowds, but he had a problem. Daniel had just counseled him, "Therefore, O king, be pleased to accept my advice: Renounce your sins by doing what is right, and your wickedness by being kind to the oppressed" (4:27). Daniel sounds just like Jesus here, talking about doing what is right and being kind.

But what was the king's reply? "Is not this the great Babylon I have built as the royal residence, by my mighty power and for the glory of my majesty?" (4:30). Doesn't sound very humble. "I'm going to make absolutely certain that everyone around here knows about Nebuchadnezzar."

But God says, "No, you won't." Daniel 4:31-32 records it: "This is what is decreed for you, King Nebuchadnezzar: Your royal authority has been taken from you. You will be driven away from people and will live with the wild animals; you will eat grass like cattle. Seven times will pass by for you until you acknowledge that the Most High is sovereign over the kingdoms of men and gives them to anyone he wishes." God has a striking way of expressing himself when people's ambitions are perverted.

Jesus said ambition is all right. You must hunger and thirst, but make absolutely certain that your ambition is not perverted. "Blessed are those who hunger and thirst for righteousness, for they will be filled" (Matt 5:6). Having been warned that ambition can be perverted, we must notice exactly what Jesus said: "Ambition must be directed." If we are to be God's men and women in a sick society, what should be our overriding ambition? It should not be hunger for power, fun, or fame. It should be to *possess* righteousness, then to *practice* righteousness, and finally to *promote* righteousness. Righteousness is to be my overwhelming ambition if I'm to be God's person on earth. I'm afraid this is not the case in all too many instances in the church. Our ambitions are basically directed in the areas of those perverted ambitions that God has categorically condemned and rebuked in the Scriptures.

Ambition to possess righteousness

What does it mean, first of all, to have an ambition to possess righteousness? In Philippians 3:6 Paul gives us an answer. He says that "as for legalistic righteousness, [he was] faultless." Paul had quite a pedigree, as he reminds us in this chapter. But he discovered he could not establish his own righteousness; so he came to God and said, "God, I've been trying be righteous, but all I am is self-righteous. Now I understand. Self-righteousness won't do. I can never establish my own righteousness. Please forgive me and give to me the righteousness of Jesus Christ." What does he mean? He means he saw himself as a person who needed the grace, mercy, and forgiveness of God. When he accepted Jesus Christ as his Savior, the righteousness of Christ was given to him.

Hunger to practice righteousness

What happens when people are in a crisis situation—aboard a hijacked airliner, a sinking ship, a runaway train? Suddenly the petty concerns of everyday life are seen in their true perspective, and the important issues become important once again. When a person believes he has forty-two more *minutes* to live, he is a different person than the one who assumes he has forty-two *years* to live. Suddenly his interests and ambitions change. He becomes realistic, just as the apostle Paul became realistic in assessing his life. He had suddenly discovered that all his earthly ambitions were really secondary, that the supreme ambition of any sane person ought to be to get right with God. Can you imagine a person not making this priority number one? When my back is to the wall I realize that my relationship to God is the most important concern I have.

When I was about twenty-five years of age, I was interviewed for a wonderful position in a bank. The official who conducted the interview (who later became my boss) asked me, "What are your ambitions?" The Lord was dealing with my life very definitely at that time, and I replied, "Sir, my ambitions are quite simply to serve God." He almost swallowed his mustache. At the end of the interview he shook hands with me and said, "Young man, it has been refreshing to meet someone who knows what he believes and why he believes it. I want you to work for me."

Many people who profess to be God's people fall short of this position in a job situation because they know the employer is not necessarily looking for someone whose ambition is to practice righteousness. They decide to be God's person in the church, but not on the job. When this happens, what do we find in the business world? Everyone is squeezed into a pale, gray, anemic mold. No one stands out as God's person.

Hunger to promote righteousness

Not only are we to be hungry to possess righteousness and to practice it, but also we are to promote righteousness. "Righteousness exalts a nation" (Prov. 14:34). We know that. This verse is often quoted. There is no such thing as a Christian nation. We can have "In God we trust" on our coins, but that doesn't make us a Christian nation. We can have a church on every corner, but that doesn't make ours a Christian nation. What exalts a nation in the sight of God is righteousness *possessed* by individuals, *practiced* by society, and *promoted* by people who have the voice.

Let's speak out for righteousness. If we do, we will encounter opposition. A worker who says to his employer, "I'm terribly sorry. I can't do what you ask because it is against my Christian principles. My ambition is to do what is right." What would the boss's reaction be? If your ambition is channeled in the right direction, that will not be your main concern. Your main concern will be to please God. Society says that right must *not* be the first priority, but rather that the easy way, the expedient action, is more important than righteousness. Even some of our country's leaders are saying that the ends justify any means. We cannot expect God to exalt a nation that has allowed its moral, ethical, and spiritual principles to erode so far that they almost no longer exist. The church of Jesus Christ has to be hungry, ambitious for that which is right. It starts with us, you and me as individuals, and spreads out like ripples in a pond.

Attitude

A society that is not only based on perverted ambition, but also has a perverted attitude, has to have problems. It is marvelous to be a Christian in a society with problems, knowing that you are God's means of rectifying the problems. Jesus said, "Blessed are the merciful"; blessed are the kind. A practicing Christian goes the extra mile and turns the other cheek. Why? Because our God is rich in mercy. If there were no other call given in Scripture, I would expect Christians to be merciful people for the very simple reason that our God is a merciful God. Grace is God giving us what we don't deserve. Mercy is God withholding from us what we *do* deserve. Merciful kindness is seeing someone reap the results of his rash actions, and being heartbroken over the pain. It's the opposite of the one who gloats over the misfortunes of others.

The church of Jesus Christ is supposed to be full of kind people, reproduced by a merciful God. Are you and I known as kind people? Or are we mainly interested in our own small world, our own concerns, our own tiny circle? A kind person will be characterized by concern more for others than for himself. He will stand out from the crowd because of his concern. This world does not like different people. But the world needs the kindness you and I can bring because our roots are in our merciful God.

Action

In Matthew 5:8 Jesus says, "Blessed are the pure in heart, for they will see God." Purity speaks of unmixed sincerity and integrity in action. Action springs from motivation, and our actions must always be evaluated in the light of what motivates them. Ananias and Sapphira did what appeared to be a magnificent thing. They sold some land and took part of the money to give to the church. This was a voluntary, benevolent, philanthropic, and spiritual action on their part. They didn't have to do it. What was wrong then? Why did God condemn them? It was because of their impure motive. They wore the facade of total dedication—conveying to their fellow church members the impression that they were giving all the money they had received. In reality, however, they were holding back part of the money. The Living Bible points out, "There was a man named Ananias (with his wife Sapphira) who sold some property, and brought only part of the money, claiming it was the full price. (His wife had agreed to this deception)" (Acts 5:1-2). Their action was good, but their motivation was impure.

One of the sad things happening in our society today is this: We evaluate people by external standards, without any knowledge of their motivations. In this sixth Beatitude Jesus was saying in effect, "Your actions will be blessed when they are more than just actions—when they are motivated by what is right and true. When you act on the basis of integrity, when there is no insincerity in you, then you are pure in heart." I know this kind of living is next to impossible in the contemporary world, but it is the lifestyle Jesus demands—and gives us the strength to perform. He knows our hearts, and while people around us can accuse us of all kinds of false motivations (because they do not know our hearts, and would condemn us even if they did), he is at our side, encouraging us along the way. In Psalm 51 David says, "Surely you desire truth in the inner parts" (v. 6). This is the way the candidate for God's blessing must pray. He must be transparent and open before God and fellow humans. This is the path to *makarios* living.

Happiness is not only the product of character; it is the promise of Christ. What does he promise? "They will be filled." The Bible teaches that the Christian life is a full life. In Colossians Paul says, "And you have been given fullness in Christ" (2:10). This expression means literally "filled full." Of what? The fullness of Christ, the fullness of the very Godhead. And out of our fullness will flow rivers of living water to the dry and barren world around us. Not only does he promise spiritual fullness, but he also promises us natural kindness, flowing from the mercy of God himself. If you want kindness, how do you get it? By showing kindness.

A word of warning. These behavior patterns I have been discussing do not *earn* salvation. They are the *evidence* of salvation. Only Christians are enabled by the risen Christ to live life *makariosly*.

MAKING IT PRACTICAL

1. What are some of the things you see people hungering and thirsting for today?

2. What are some practical ways we can keep our ambition focused on what is good and right?

3. Why should Christians be merciful people?

4. What does it mean to you to be pure in heart?

5. What are some specific ways that we as Christians can try to keep our motivations pure and focused on what is right?

Blessed are the peacemakers, for they will be called sons of God.

Blessed are those who are persecuted because of righteousness, for theirs is the kingdom of heaven.

Blessed are you when people insult you, persecute you and falsely say all kinds of evil against you because of me. Rejoice and be glad, because great is your reward in heaven, for in the same way they persecuted the prophets who were before you.

Matthew 5:9-12

4
Peacemaking

No passage in the whole Bible speaks more succinctly, more powerfully, more challengingly than the Sermon on the Mount. Whatever one's interpretation of this passage might be, it unquestionably enunciates how God wants his people to act.

So far we have seen that happiness is a product of character, and that happiness is the promise of Christ. In this chapter we will deal with Christ's statement that happiness is the product of a character that pursues peace and persists under persecution.

At first glance there seems to be a conflict here. How can we talk about peace and persecution in the same breath? How can a Christian know the same kind of happiness in peace as he does in persecution? We usually think of peace as the absence of persecution. "If I'm at peace, there won't be persecution; and if there's persecution, there won't be peace." Not so. Our understanding of peace usually assumes that peace is the absence of hostility. Again not so. Look at the international situation. In many areas of the world—for example the Middle East—people have been coexisting under what might be called a very uneasy peace, punctuated by wars, for years. While people are not shooting at one another, they are considered at peace. But in many cases it's a shaky truce at best—not peace.

When God talks about peace, he does not mean merely the absence of overt hostility. He is dealing with the ability to triumph over hostility and know a quality of divine life in the midst of it. It is possible to know peace when all around you there is war. It takes someone in whom the Spirit of God is working to be at peace when everything is going wrong. On that basis it is not a contradiction to say that blessedness is the product of character that pursues peace and yet persists under persecution. The two can live together.

The Character That Pursues Peace

Let's first look at the character that pursues peace. There are four areas to note: the passion for peace, the price of peace, the pursuit of peace, and the prize of peace.

The Passion for peace

What do I mean by the passion for peace? I believe a real impact will be made on society through the life of one who passionately desires peace, who really longs to see peace, and to produce it in his or her own life. Many Christians lack this heartfelt desire for peace. They prefer to settle for mutual coexistence. This is not the true peace of which God speaks. God wants people who have a passion for peace to verbalize their faith. One of the basic characteristics of Christian character in a non-Christian world is a desire to see other people discover that peace.

In 2 Corinthians 5:20 Paul indicates that our passion for peace will be primarily a passion for spiritual peace: "We are therefore Christ's ambassadors, as though God were making his appeal through us. We implore you on Christ's behalf: Be reconciled to God." What is Paul praying? He is sharing a passionate desire for men and women to discover spiritual peace. Paul is a striking example of what I mean by a person who has a passion for peace. Jesus said, "Blessed are the peacemakers." It takes a special kind of dedication to produce a man or woman who is burning with a passion for others to be reconciled to God. Blessed are the peacemakers who are making peace between God and individuals.

Not only are we to have a passion for spiritual peace, but we are also to have a passion for social peace. Paul spells it out for us in Romans 12:17-18: "Do not repay anyone evil for evil. Be careful to do what is right in the eyes of everybody. If it is possible, as far as it depends on you, live at peace with everyone." Verse 18 contains two tremendously important clauses which take this concept out of the realm of the idealistic and bring it down to the realm of the realistic. Paul doesn't say bluntly, "Live at peace with everyone." There's no way you can live at peace with some people. No matter what you do, they will not accept you. But Paul isn't talking idealistically here; he is speaking realistically. He says, *If it is possible, as far as it depends on you,* live at peace with everyone." What is our typical reaction when someone wrongs us or takes advantage of us? Retaliation! It really isn't surprising that our hostile world discounts our Christianity. So many times our attitudes and our behavior are identical to theirs.

Let's bring it even closer to home. This passion for peace would make a vital difference in many marriages. The lack of peace is one of the chronic problems in American society today—marriages are severed by warfare rather than drawn together by mutual love.

What would happen in industry if the overriding desire was for peace? What if the Christian in industry would really put this principle of peacemaking into practice?

This command implies a passion for personal peace as well. In Matthew 5:24 (later in his Sermon on the Mount) Jesus said, "Leave your gift there in front of the altar. First go and be reconciled to your brother; then come and offer your gift." Often we Christians go to a worship service with an unprepared heart. We bring both our gift and our resentment. As Christians we are responsible for our own attitudes. If I have anything against another Christian, or if that person has anything against me, that should be confessed and the slate cleared before I come before God in worship. I am not responsible for the attitude of the other person, but I am responsible to do all I can, by confession and a desire for peace, to make sure nothing separating me from another person will come between me and my God.

The Price of peace

"God was pleased . . . through him to reconcile to himself all things, whether things on earth or things in heaven, by making peace through his blood, shed on the cross" (Col. 1:19-20). Paul is speaking here of the same kind of peacemaking that Jesus was talking about in the Sermon on the Mount. How did Jesus make peace? Through his blood, shed on the cross. The price of the spiritual peace between God and man, the cost of reconciliation, was the blood of God's own Son! This is the value God has placed upon peace. If I do not have a passion for peace and a deep-seated desire to see others come under the blanket of that reconciliation, am I trampling underfoot that precious blood, shed to pay for that peace?

The price of peace is more than blood shed; it is also barriers broken down. Often we fail to have peace with other people simply because we feel threatened by them. Our natural reaction when we are threatened is to build defenses, barriers between ourselves and the source of the threat. Once we have defenses, we naturally assume a defensive attitude.

If there are barriers between me and another person, I don't solve the problem by attacking the other person's defenses. To solve it I must tear down my own defenses. I make myself vulnerable. One of the reasons peace is not restored in many relationships is simply this: We want others to lower their defenses before we do anything about ours. *If I lower my guard,* we reason, *he'll get me.* This is the crux of the matter. This is the heart of the peacemaker who is willing to pay the price for peace.

If I'm going to build a bridge between myself and another person, I have to start on my side. Have you ever seen a bridge built? The builders start with a solid structure on each side of the body of water they want to span. Then a thin little cable is sent across, securely fastened at one side, and secured at the other. That is the basis for the bridge--a thin little cable starting from one side but eventually connected at both ends. That's the way it is with peacemaking. It must start with me. That is what Jesus was calling for when he said, "Blessed are the peacemakers."

When does peace begin to be made? When blood is shed, when barriers are broken down. Why don't people live in peace? Because each one is waiting for the other to bring the cable. And no bridge is ever made. Pay the price. Shed the blood. Break the barriers. Build the bridges. This is the price of peace.

The Pursuit of peace

In 1 Peter 3:10-11 the apostle writes, "Whoever would love life and see good days must keep his tongue from evil and his lips from deceitful speech. He must turn from evil and do good; *he must seek peace and pursue it*" (italics mine). The King James Version uses the word *ensue,* which is the same word that is translated "persecute" in Matthew 5. It means to relentlessly hunt a thing down. Saul of Tarsus was a persecutor. Indeed, he was on his way to Damascus to do some serious hunting when he met the Master. This is the way we are to pursue peace. In the vernacular we would probably say, "Kill them with kindness."

Let me point out and lay to rest some misconceptions about the pursuit of peace. No Christian is given the right to be at peace with evil. There is no such thing in the divine economy as "peace at any price." If God had been satisfied with peace at any price, he would have found a cheaper price than the Cross. He would have come to terms with Satan and sin in a less costly manner. We are to pursue peace—but never by settling for evil or error.

One of the tragedies in the church today is the existence of "peace" at the expense of truth. We can never build peace by accepting evil. We can never build peace by condoning error.

This leads to the matter of church discipline. There are times when discipline must be exercised and error must be isolated to view. Years ago my idea of a peacemaker was a skinny, anemic little guy who allowed people to trample all over him. Frankly, that's not my way! But to be a peacemaker in the biblical sense is anything but like my former impression. It's a rough, challenging occupation. We cannot have a healthy church if our idea of church discipline is "peace at any price." Problems in the church must be dealt with in love, but with firmness.

The fruit of the Spirit is love, joy, and peace (among other characteristics). How do I pursue peace? In the enabling power of the Holy Spirit. Don't think it's an automatic process, however. Just because the Spirit is in me does not mean I'm automatically a peacemaker. It simply means that now I'm free to *pursue* peace. Now I'm free to do something about this indwelling spiritual conviction out in the world, where I as a Christian must make a difference.

The Prize of peace

The blessings of God are contentment, joy, happiness, all deeply rooted in a right relationship to God. These are the ingredients of the peacemaker's life. This *makarios* life is the prize of peace. A sense of fulfillment that overflows the spirit is the prize of peace. Notice the last part of this Beatitude: "for they will be called sons of God" (Matt. 5:9). Not *become* children of God—that happens when we accept Christ. We become children of God by receiving Jesus Christ. No, to be *called* children of God means to become known as a child of God because of our peacemaking attitude. It means nothing less than the recognition of a hostile world.

The Character That Persists

This leads us right back to the subject of the earlier part of this chapter. Happiness is not only the product of a character that pursues peace, but also the product of a character that persists under persecution. Jesus put it in perspective for us: "Do not suppose that I have come to bring peace to the earth. I did not come to bring peace, but a sword" (Matt. 10:34). This verse links the two together—peace and persecution. Remember the adoration that surrounded the manger at the birth of Christ—and the anger that came down from Herod just a short time later? Think of the adulation Christ received on Palm Sunday—and the hatred that descended on him later that same week. The kind of peace that Jesus came to bring—some people welcome it, but others are antagonistic toward him and the reconciliation he offers.

The same kind of reception awaits you and me as Christians as we go out into the arena of the world. If we go out where the action is, if we get involved in the battle, we will discover that our peace will lead us into persecution. Some husbands and wives will meet persecution when they live Christ-controlled lives in their homes. Some workers will encounter persecution on the job because of their outspoken faith.

We have all heard of the great Tribulation, and a battle has been raging for generations as to what this event really means and when it is going to take place. In all honesty I must say that much of the interest in the subject of the Tribulation appears to stem from a desire to make sure we will not go through it! This hardly seems to be the attitude that leads to blessing according to our Lord's teaching. We should not be concentrating on avoiding pressure but rather ensuring that we live *"makariosly"* under pressure.

What about the persecution our Christian brothers and sisters endured behind the Iron Curtain? I would say theirs was the deepest of tribulation experiences. I have a friend in Czechoslovakia who speaks five languages fluently, including Japanese. He had to give up his business because he would not follow the communist party line when his country was taken over. He now works as a hotel porter. Another friend was a doctor of law. After the communist takeover he became a church secretary. Today there are many more such examples in China, the Middle East, and other parts of Asia.

We can expect tribulation to come upon those who choose to stand firm for Christ—even ourselves. The Beatitude says, "Blessed are you *when* people insult you and persecute you." (Matt. 5:11, italics mine). Notice, it is *when,* not if. Persecution is coming upon us; make no mistake on that score. Our identification with Christ automatically means alienation from Satan. Our identification with truth automatically means alienation from lies. And alienation is a close relative of persecution.

When does the blessing come? When I persist under persecution. Why are so few Christians blessed—and so many singularly unblessed? The moment persecution comes, they quit under its pressure. May that never be said of you and me!

MAKING IT PRACTICAL

1. When a person passionately desires peace, how does it show in his or her life?

2. As you look around you, what are some examples you see of situations where spiritual, social, and personal peace are needed?

3. Where does peace begin? How does a person begin to be a peacemaker in these situations?

4. What is the number-one reason it is so difficult to be a peace-maker?

5. What are some specific and practical ways we can seek and relentlessly pursue peace in our world today?

You are the salt of the earth. But if the salt loses its saltiness, how can it be made salty again? It is no longer good for anything, except to be thrown out and trampled by men.

Matthew 5:13

5

Salt of the Earth

Having outlined the principles and qualities that make Christians distinctive, the Lord Jesus now goes on to give a striking picture of what it really means to behave as a Christian. In describing the Christian as the salt of the earth, Jesus provides a powerful illustration of the impact and impression Christians should be making on the society in which they live.

We are responsible to live out our Christianity where God has placed us, to behave distinctively as Christians where we are. The size of our influence is not our concern. Christ said, "You *are* the salt." The question is not whether we are salt or not—the question is whether we are *functioning* as salt or not functioning.

The Status of Being Salt

What does it mean to be salt? Jesus isn't asking for volunteers here. He is saying, "Whether you want to be or not, you are salt." This means that God has a plan for each one of us to fulfill. Each of us is to function as salt in the little piece of geography to which he has called us: our neighborhood, the office, or wherever we are. We are to make an impact upon that area of influence where God has placed us. How can any Christian be bored or blase after realizing this truth? How can we be less than excited and exhilarated by this call to the "normal Christian life"?

Salt is necessary

An important aspect of this whole concept of being salt is that the world around us needs Christians to be salt. Just because we Christians are forgiven and on our way to heaven, that does not mean that's all there is! Our role isn't to sit back and wait for the bus to pick us up. God knows how critically important we are to our world. If we are to fulfill our God-given role as salt, we can never settle down to a *mundane* existence. Salt is desperately needed. Let me illustrate.

When I was in the Marines, we used to go on speed marches. On a speed march you simply run all the way. When you come to a hill, you run twice as fast! All we had to eat on those marches was salt, actual chunks of it. Perspiration would blind us, but as long as we had the salt, we could go on. Without it we could not survive.

In the Middle East, salt is one of the most precious commodities available. Life functions require salt. It is the very sustenance of life itself; and in Jesus' day as now, salt was vital and pivotal in the lifestyle of the people.

What an exciting concept! You and I as Christians are vital to the world around us. We can say, "O God, if this little piece of geography is to survive as you intended, if the people in it are to survive, it actually needs me as its salt." That gives Christianity a totally new dimension. The saltiness of the Christian is necessary for the world's survival.

Salt is distinctive

Salt is also distinctive in nature. Christians are to stand out from the crowd. They are to be different in their approach to life. Not only should our lifestyle be distinctive; we should also serve as the world's "early warning system." When the world around us seems bent on its own destruction, or indifferent to its own danger, we Christians are to stand up and be counted, not just for the sake of being different—but to be the "salt" that preserves and purifies. We march to a different drummer; we live by a different set of principles. The world around us must know this. The little section of society in which we circulate takes a different view of life than we do. There are two basic views: God's view and man's view. We represent God, and the world desperately needs this view.

Salt is abrasive

Not only is salt imperative for survival and distinctive in nature; it is also abrasive in character. Let me illustrate what I mean from the Bible.

A certain little town is described in Judges 18:7:

> So the five men left and came to Laish, where they saw that the people were living in safety, like the Sidonians, unsuspecting and secure. And since their land lacked nothing, they were prosperous. Also, they lived a long way from the Sidonians and had no relationship with anyone else.

Everyone in Laish was living comfortably, lacking nothing and possessing wealth. In the face of an approaching enemy, they remained unconcerned. They who were living comfortably perished comfortably! If only there had been one man who had stood to his feet and shouted, "Fools! Wake up!" The people would have been upset at one who rocked the boat this way. They might have called him an oddball. But he might have saved their lives.

This is the kind of abrasive character we Christians are to have. We are to confront people around us with the truth in total contrast to the lies that are lulling them to sleep. That's what it means to be a Christian. This is the status of being salt.

The Significance of Being Salt

What did Jesus' statement concerning the Christian's responsibility to be salt mean to his immediate hearers—the people of Galilee? Those people knew immediately what he was talking about. For them, salt was not something in a shiny silver shaker on the dinner table.

Salt preserves

To the people of that day salt was primarily a preservative vital to their way of life. Once they caught a fish, they had to get it to market. The only way to get it there in marketable condition was to salt it and pack it between layers of salt so they could carry it with them to Jerusalem, where it could be sold as fresh as when they caught it. Salt arrested corruption; it kept fish fresh and edible.

We Christians today are to arrest the corruption in our society. Unfortunately, many Christians do not even know what is going on in the world around them; they are unaware of the terrible conditions that exist unchecked. This is one of the reasons, I believe, why we are not making a difference in the world around us.

On the contrary, Paul was aware of his world when he wrote, "For the message of the cross is foolishness to those who are perishing, but to us who are being saved it is the power of God" (1 Cor. 1:18). What has that to do with being salt? "Perishing" aptly describes the condition of society today. The same word used in the original Greek for "perishing" is also used for "lost." People around us are lost, victims of a disease known as sin, which causes their lostness and corruption. Jesus called for his followers to be the salt that would halt that condition. If the corruption is not arrested, those who are now in the process of perishing will one day finally, ultimately, and irrevocably perish for all eternity. We Christians are placed in the midst of this perishing, corrupt society to do what we can to halt the corruption, to stem the tide of godlessness all around us.

There are many ways for us to do this. Some feel it can be done through local government. Others think national politics can make the difference. Still others feel that by being involved in helping agencies of one kind or another, they can turn the tide. But what is the basic way to do it? We must get at the root of corruption in the individuals. Their condition must be changed. Instead of being in the process of perishing, they must be saved. The problem is basically spiritual, even though it has social implications and ramifications. That is why the Christian's main concern as salt is to arrest the corruption in society by being the instrument to bring individuals in society to a knowledge of Christ and an experience of salvation. You and I are the means God can use to arrest the corruption in the world around us. Are we functioning as salt?

Salt confirms the promise

Salt has another meaning in the Scriptures. Even today in the Middle East business agreements and other arrangements are sealed with salt. Numbers 18:19 provides the background of this usage:

> Whatever is set aside from the holy offerings the Israelites present to the LORD I give to you and your sons and daughters as your regular share. It is an everlasting covenant of salt before the LORD for both you and your offspring.

This "covenant of salt" is a symbol that had real meaning for those who heard Jesus speaking on the mount. What is the meaning of salt in this context? It is a means of introducing the covenant between God and his people. As we share our experience with Christ, we are passing along this "covenant of salt," this promise of truth. People can "bite into" our experience to test its reality, allowing us the tremendous privilege of being salt to our society. We show to the world, which desperately needs our message, that God is prepared to make a new covenant through the blood of his Son. In 2 Corinthians 3:6 Paul tells us God "has made us competent as ministers of a new covenant—not of the letter but of the Spirit; for the letter kills, but the Spirit gives life."

Are you and I as Christians truly functioning as salt? Are many people around us coming to grips with the fact that it is possible for

God and human beings to be reconciled through Christ's blood, shed on the cross? Do they know it is possible for lostness, corruption, and alienation to be done away with? That's what it means to be salt.

Salt has positive and negative power

This brings us to a third significance of salt. In the Old Testament we are told that it was a military practice in destroying the enemy to sow that city with salt: "All that day Abimelech pressed his attack against the city until he had captured it and killed its people. Then he destroyed the city and scattered salt over it" (Judg. 9:45). This was done so that nothing would ever grow in the area again. It was totally and utterly destroyed. This is the way a Christian should function. Our life, our testimony, our very presence should be a positive witness for Christ, but it should be a negative condemnation to the person who refuses to believe.

Writing to the Corinthians, Paul makes this point: "For we are to God the aroma of Christ among those who are being saved and those who are perishing. To the one we are the smell of death; to the other, the fragrance of life" (2 Cor. 2:15-16). I believe this is the reason many Christians fall by the wayside. They want to live comfortably like the people of Laish. They don't want to upset or perturb anyone. But some people need to be upset and perturbed. What do we do when we see a blind man walking toward a cliff? Do we keep quiet because we don't want to disturb or frighten him? If we do, we're guilty of criminal negligence! If we honestly believe in the corrupting influence of sin and the condemnation of God upon it, then we are responsible to warn the world around us of its danger. Our very quality of life should be a beacon of hope to them. That's what it means to be salt.

The Lord Jesus invested a remarkable power in his disciples, the people to whom he was talking here on the mount. John tells us that Jesus said, "If you forgive anyone his sins, they are forgiven; if you do not forgive them, they are not forgiven" (20:23). I know there are many interpretations of this, but I believe Jesus was saying simply this: "If you go out into society and tell people, 'My dear friend, if you refuse to repent, to bow your head and heart before a holy God, if you refuse to acknowledge Jesus Christ as your Savior and Lord, on the authority of the Word of God, you are lost and bound for a Christless eternity,' I will support you from heaven itself." This is what Jesus' words here in John mean to me. Jesus was asking his disciples to function as salt—to affirm his message of condemnation for sin, and salvation for the repentant.

Salt purifies

Salt is also a purifier. If you've ever had an open cut, you know how salt in that wound made it sting. But it also made it clean. That's another aspect of salt's function—to administer cleansing. There is an interesting reference to the cleansing power of salt in Ezekiel 16:4: "On the day you were born your cord was not cut, nor were you washed with water to make you clean, nor were you rubbed with salt." Salt was used here as part of the cleansing process. What a beautiful, challenging thing it is to be a Christian in the world today. We are to be a means of cleansing. We're not to think of ourselves as better or greater than others because of this call. No, we are servants of the living God as we fulfill this function of being salt.

Salt enhances flavor

Job asked the question "Is tasteless food eaten without salt, or is there flavor in the white of an egg?" (6:6) Did you ever try to eat something that had not been salted to your taste? Flat and unexciting, wasn't it? I'm afraid that's the way many of us Christians come through to people around us. It's what Jesus was referring to in Luke 14:34-35 when he said, "Salt is good, but if it loses its saltiness, how can it be made salty again? It is fit neither for the soil nor for the manure pile; it is thrown out" (Luke 14:34-35).

We Christians have no business being boring. Our function is to add flavor and excitement. Jesus was saying in effect, "Does this world have to go on the way it is without salt? Can't we have some salt around here, please, that will add a beautiful touch to the whole thing?" If I as a Christian am boring and dull, if I'm not adding flavor to life around me, I'm not fulfilling my function as salt.

When I was in the Marines, I was the only one in my group who didn't booze it up. Night after night the others would invite me to go out drinking with them, and I would regularly say no to their invitation. Do you know what happened? I became nursemaid and helper, putting them to bed, helping them cope with their hangovers. At least I added a little touch of difference to the situation. In fact, as the months went by, one by one many of those Marines came to know Christ.

The Seriousness of Being Salt

This brings us to the "but" of our verse: "You are the salt of the earth. *But* if the salt loses its saltiness, . . ." Here Jesus is getting around to the importance of fulfilling our function as salt. There is danger, disgrace, and possible disaster here in terms of our Christian testimony. The possibility that the salt may lose its savor was hinted at by Paul in Romans: "Although they claimed to be wise, they became fools" (1:22). Nothing about salt here, is there? In the Greek it's the same word as Jesus used when he pointed out that it is possible for the salt to lose its savor. In Galilee, where Jesus lived at this time, a cheap grade of salt was used for packing fish. Once it lost its saltiness it was useless. If it was spread on the ground, nothing would grow. If it was thrown in the water, it just made the water dirty. This savorless salt was not good for anything. Jesus was saying, "If you're not careful, salt of the earth, you will lose your edge, your distinctiveness, your abrasiveness, your power, your very reason for being." You will become "fools" as Paul pointed out in Romans 1 and 1 Corinthians 1. Freely translated, what Jesus was saying is this: "If the salt fools around, it will lose its impact."

Are we as Christians functioning or just fooling around? We can fool around by being more concerned for spiritual complacency than for changing the world for Christ. We can fool around by being more interested in social conformity than spiritual impact. We can also fool around by being more confused morally than any Christian has a right to be. We don't help anyone out of confusion if we are confused ourselves.

I've heard the term "good for nothing" applied to a variety of people. But Jesus applies it to saltless Christians! It's possible for a Christian to fool around so much that he's good for nothing but to be trampled underfoot. His testimony is worthless. Fellow Christian, I want to be salty as a Christian, don't you?

MAKING IT PRACTICAL

1. What did Jesus mean when he told his disciples that they were "the salt of the earth"?

2. What are some of the characteristics of salt that we as Christians are also supposed to have?

3. Discuss some of the uses for salt and their bearing upon the Christian life. For example, how can Christians function as a preservative?

4. What are some ways that we as Christians can purify and add flavor?

5. What does it mean when we say the salt has "lost its saltiness"? How can we as Christians be sure that we stay "salty"?

You are the light of the world. A city on a hill cannot be hidden. Neither do people light a lamp and put it under a bowl. Instead they put it on its stand, and it gives light to everyone in the house. In the same way, let your light shine before men, that they may see your good deeds and praise your Father in heaven.

Matthew 5:14-16

6

Light of the World

Jesus uses another graphic illustration to portray the healthy Christian life. He is talking about distinctive Christianity, supernormal living, in Matthew 5:14-16.

Knowing what to believe is one thing. Knowing how to behave is an entirely different matter. But the two are closely related. We need a knowledge of Christian doctrine to understand not only what we believe but also why we believe it. But then we need to know what to do about what we believe. So far we have discovered that if Christian behavior, morality, ethics, and living are not abrasive, then they are certainly not what God intended them to be.

We Christians are not only to be "the salt of the earth"; we are also to be "the light of the world." In this chapter we will examine what Jesus meant by his use of the term *light*. Then we will deal with the expectation—what did Jesus expect to happen in our lives because we are "light"? Finally, we will look at his exhortation to us to "let our light shine."

As we pointed out in chapter 5, Jesus is not looking for volunteers or raised hands. If he had been, he would have opened his call by saying, "Who would like to be the light of the world?" And he did not say, "What the world needs is lights." He was not offering options; he was making plain statements: "You *are* light" and "You *are* salt." The question is not whether you want to be or not. It is, Will you function or not? If salt functions, it will not lose its savor. Light cannot function as a light if it is hidden under a bucket. The Lord would say to us today as he did to those other disciples, "Look, I'm going to produce in you a distinctive behavior, a totally new way of living that will be as abrasive, effective, and unique as salt on the earth. And I'm going to so work in your life that you're going to be as noticeable as a light shining in a dark place." He made it clear that the possibility exists of salt losing its saltiness and light being hidden. But you and I are the salt and the light, and if salt doesn't function and light doesn't shine, then we are failing to be what Jesus called us to be. And we are failing to reach our desperately needy world. I am convinced that unless the church of Jesus Christ really begins to fulfill its function as light and salt, we cannot expect the gospel of Jesus Christ to make an impact on the world.

What Did Jesus Mean?

What did Jesus mean when he said, "You are the light of the world"? I think he meant we are the continuation, clarification, and coordination of his ministry.

We continue what he started

First of all, I think he was talking about his disciples having a continuation ministry. If we look at what he said in John 8 and 9, this truth begins to emerge: "While I am in the world, I am the light of the world" (9:5); "I am the light of the world. Whoever follows me will never walk in darkness, but will have the light of life" (8:12). Now in Matthew 5:14 he is saying, "You are the light of the world." Put those three passages together and what do you have? We are *now* what Christ was *then*. While he was here, *he* was the light. Now that he is gone, *we* are the light.

We Christians are here in the world to be, through our body universal, local, and individual, nothing more or less than the outshining of the glory of Jesus Christ to a world that lives in darkness. Do you know what our world should be saying simply because it is seeing the lives of Christians? It ought to be saying, "We who live in darkness have seen a great light!" You and I are the lights of the world. If we only begin to understand our lives as a continuation of his ministry begun 1900 years ago, how can we condone complacent behavior and excuse our lack of involvement? We are a continuation of his ministry.

We become an example for others to follow

Being the "light of the world" gives us a clarification ministry as well. When he made the statement, "I am the light of the world," he went on to say, "Whoever follows me will not walk in darkness, but will have the light of life." When Christians continue the ministry that Christ initiated, we will have followers as he did. People today must find in us such reality, such revelation and truth, such exhilarating excitement, that they will have their darkness banished and begin to understand what it really means to live.

Does that idea frighten you? Does it sound heretical? I believe we have, in the life of the apostle Paul, a good precedent for thinking this way. He was actually able to say, "Follow my example, as I follow the example of Christ" (1 Cor. 11:1). What was he saying? I follow Jesus Christ, and he is the light of the world. Through his ministry, his life in me, I am becoming something of what he is. Therefore, if you can't see him, look at me. You'll begin to find in and through me something of the glorious person of Jesus Christ. And you can begin to come to grips with him through the ministry I'm having among you.

I find that concept almost terrifying, but that's what Jesus is saying. It's terrifying because it suddenly means that as a Christian, I'm inevitably a marked person. Because of my profession as a Christian, others are going to follow me. And if my performance does not equal that profession, if my action is not adequate, I will lead them in the wrong way.

You and I are the light of the world. As Christians we are to be "little Christs." Do some look at us and say, "If that's Christianity, you can keep it"? In many instances people have been turned against the church because of the behavior of people in church. They were impressed with Jesus Christ through some unusual experience, but were later singularly unimpressed with those who profess to be his followers. Why? For this very simple reason: We have failed to recognize that we are what he is. We continue what he began. There should be no conflict between our lives and his, no break in his ministry. We should so grasp his principles, and so enjoy his life, that his life will flow through us and out to others, performing this clarifying ministry.

This light-giving ministry is the reason we are here. I wonder how the church of Jesus Christ degenerated into a group of people just sitting around congratulating themselves that they are on the way to heaven. What a tragedy!

We are to bring order and beauty to the world

We also have a ministry of coordination. The word here translated as "world" is different from the word *earth* found in verse 13. You will recall that the word used in verse 13 is used to mean our own little piece of geography, and we're told to be salt in that place. Here in verse 14, the word is *kosmos,* meaning "order." The Greek idea of beauty was order. This is the same word from which we get the word *cosmetic.* The essence of beauty in the Greek mind was order, balance. God created a system that functions beautifully. He created order and beauty, and man spoiled it. I'm not referring only to what Adam did in the garden; I'm thinking, too, of the ecological mess our world is in today. Because man's greed has destroyed the once perfect balance of nature, we're on the brink of ecological disaster. Even the vast regions of space that surround our planet are polluted by man's idiocy. God made the cosmos, and man made chaos.

What is God saying to us? He says, "What I want is order and beauty. And I'm going to bring it by shining through the chaos as the light of the world. You are that light." If I'm going to be that person whose life demonstrates the harmony of God's creation, then coordination must characterize my life, not chaos. That divine quality is going to spill over into my home, my neighborhood, my world. I'm the light of cosmos, the light of order, *the* light.

Does that concept frighten you with its sheer weight of responsibility? I'm frightened by it—but I must recognize my accountability to be a clarifier and a coordinator and to continue the ministry Christ began.

Let me paint a picture. Our world is in darkness. Its ships are breaking up on the heavy seas. The storm is rapidly engulfing the vessels. People are going down, and they don't even know where they are. They're lost and confused. Overlooking them is a lighthouse—the church of Jesus Christ, or even more personally, each individual Christian. We are to be steadfast, immovable, inflexible, shining brightly, a light in a dark place. That's what Jesus is calling for here.

Not long ago I was talking to a young lady who expressed her dissatisfaction with her living arrangements. She told me she wanted to move. I asked her why.

"Well," she said, "I'm the only Christian there."

"I still don't understand why you want to move," I replied.

"Because I'm the only Christian there."

"I still don't understand," I persisted.

"It's such a dark place," she explained further.

"It would seem to me that the darker the place, the brighter the light that's needed," I answered.

That's what it means to consolidate, to be a reference point, to be a light in the world. The more confusion there is, the greater the need for a solid foundation, one who knows the truth and stands upright for it.

C. T. Studd had an interesting limerick:

Some people like to live within
the sound of church or chapel bell.
I'd rather run a rescue shop
within a yard of hell.

They say that Nero fiddled while Rome burned. I wonder how many Christians are fooling around today while people around them are going to hell. You and I are a city set on a hill, the light of the world. We're to be a beacon light to rescue hell-bound sinners around us.

What Does Jesus Expect of Christians?

Jesus said, "Neither do people light a lamp and put it under a bowl. Instead they put it on its stand, and it gives light to everyone in the house." (v. 15). A simple expectation is expressed here: that bowls will be removed and candle stands discovered. There are two definite "bowls," two definite obstacles to our shining as lights: the bowl of indifference and the bowl of inconsistency.

I'm coming down pretty hard here, but one thing that really irritates me is an indifferent Christian—because he's the greatest living contradiction you can find. Indifference and Christians do not belong together. Yet who among us can say truthfully that we don't show indifference every day of our lives? In so doing, we're putting our lights under a bowl; we're a contradiction in terms. And inconsistency is perhaps the most common means of hiding our testimony.

What's the difference between putting our light under a bowl and placing it on a stand? A "stand" Christian accepts every opportunity to shine, whereas a "bowl" Christian hides his light every time he is faced with an opportunity to shine. A stand gives the light a very strategic position. As Christians we're not just to blink and twinkle. No, we're to look for the best and most strategic place to function as lights. That's the expectation Jesus has for us. "Get out from under your bowl, and climb up on your stand!" he says in no uncertain terms.

If I'm to obey his command, I will look for the most strategic place, then discover how to shed the most light possible from that place. The expectation is that I will avoid the hidden obstacles, accept the opportunities that come my way, and acknowledge my obligations. That's the way I can let my light shine.

What Is Jesus Strongly Urging Us to Do?

Now, having explained his statement and outlined his expectations, Jesus says, "Let your light shine before men, that they may see your good deeds and praise your Father in heaven" (v. 16). To put it in today's terminology, Jesus is saying, "Okay, everybody, get out there and shine!"

First of all, what is to be the *method* of shining? Jesus spells it out quite clearly and unequivocally—works! That'll shake some of us evangelicals. No, we're not saved *by* good works, but that doesn't mean we can forget about them. We're saved *unto* good works. James explained the rationale behind that arrangement:

In the same way, faith by itself, if it is not accompanied by action, is dead.

But someone will say, "You have faith; I have deeds."

Show me your faith without deeds, and I will show you my faith by what I do. *James 2:17-18*

To paraphrase James, "If my faith doesn't work, it is highly suspect. It can shout; it can preach; it can pound the pulpit. But if it doesn't work, it's dead." What kind of works? *Good* works. Good works are works that are visible. That doesn't mean just being a nice guy, a good neighbor, a law-abiding citizen. It means much more—standing out from the world around you like a light on a candlestick, a city on a hill.

Next, let's look at the *means* of shining. First, "kindle the flame!" If you have a flicker for a flame, tell the Lord, "I must admit I've been a pretty pathetic light, Lord. All I've produced so far is smoke. Instead of giving people light, I'm afraid I've offended their nostrils. Set me alight!"

Then "trim the wick"—carefully and regularly work on your lifestyle to remove the grimy deposit of less-than-satisfactory living.

Thirdly, "replenish the oil"—make sure that you are drawing deeply from the God-given resources made available to you in the Holy Spirit.

Finally, what is your *motivation?* Does a candle shine merely to be seen? Do candles shine to illuminate other candles? Candles shine to banish darkness. Did you ever see a Christian whose overriding ambition was simply to be seen? Such a person has a real problem. There's too much darkness out there to be concerned about self-glorification. Our works are to glorify our Father in heaven. That's why we are to be lights in the world!

MAKING IT PRACTICAL

1. What does it mean to be "the light of the world"?

2. How do you think the church today is doing at continuing the ministry Jesus started? How do you think we could do better?

3. How do you react to the idea that people will want to "follow our example as we follow the example of Christ"?

4. Do you agree with the author's statement that "the darker the place, the brighter the light that's needed"? If so, what are the implications for your life?

5. What are some ways we can be sure that our good works cause people to be reminded of how wonderful God is rather than how wonderful we are?

Do not think that I have come to abolish the Law or the Prophets; I have not come to abolish them but to fulfill them. I tell you the truth, until heaven and earth disappear, not the smallest letter, not the least stroke of a pen, will by any means disappear from the Law until everything is accomplished. Anyone who breaks one of the least of these commandments and teaches others to do the same will be called least in the kingdom of heaven, but whoever practices and teaches these commands will be called great in the kingdom of heaven. For I tell you that unless your righteousness surpasses that of the Pharisees and the teachers of the Law, you will certainly not enter the kingdom of heaven.

Matthew 5:17-20

7

The Moral Law

The biblical teaching that God provided an absolute moral standard has been neglected in our modern and "enlightened" day. And the results are clearly seen in the moral chaos all around us. A clear restatement of God's moral law is imperative at this particular time. Many people are deeply concerned about the great upsurge of immorality in our day. Frankly, I'm not as concerned about immorality as I am about the rise of amorality. Immorality is the breaking of a moral standard, but amorality simply says that there is no such thing as a moral standard. It seems to me that this attitude is our real danger in the world today.

We live in a society that says there are no absolute moral standards. A classic example is the development of conflicting pornography legislation. The highest court in the land copped out by saying that it is up to the local area to determine what is pornographic, throwing the whole situation into confusion.

Society is saying, in effect, "It's really up to everyone to decide his own moral standards. And if you don't have any, that's all right, too. Just don't bother anyone else, because we're all free to make up our own minds!"

This is in total opposition to the clear teachings of the Scriptures. The Bible tells us that God is the author of morality, that he is a moral being, and that he has legislated certain moral standards, without which no society can exist in right relationship with him or each other. An absence of a solid moral foundation is an invitation to moral chaos.

The Importance of the Moral Law

Early in his Sermon on the Mount, the Lord Jesus came out in strong defense of the moral law of God. In Matthew 5:17 he said, "Do not think that I have come to abolish the Law or the Prophets; I have not come to abolish them but to fulfill them." The law to which he was referring here was the law God revealed to Moses on Mount Sinai, which we commonly call the Ten Commandments, recorded in Exodus 20.

Enacted by God

First of all, the importance of the moral law lies in the fact that it was enacted by God. "And God spoke all these words: 'I am the LORD your God, who brought you out of Egypt, out of the land of slavery' " (Exod. 20:1-2). Following this introduction God goes on to give the ten basic statements that are still the core of his moral law, and just as relevant for us today as they were for those people to whom they were given thousands of years ago. One of the crying needs of our world is simply to be reminded that God is a moral being who has given us an uncompromising moral standard that relates and applies to life today.

There are two important truths for us to see in this moral law. First, it is a revelation of the being of God. He says, "I am the Lord your God." Some people seem to think they can break the law simply because they do not like the lawmakers! Such people are putting the Lawmaker into a class with themselves, making him no better than themselves. God nips that kind of thinking in the bud when he identifies himself right here at the outset. No one can adopt this kind of an attitude toward God, for the very preamble of his law reveals that he is the one from whom all things come.

Secondly, God makes it clear that he is not about to share his glory with anyone. The first commandment states unequivocally, "You shall have no other gods before me" (Exod. 20:3). This is the Supreme Being speaking, and he is the One who led Israel out of Egypt. His law is a legitimate requirement of those he has created and sustained.

After firmly establishing his identity as God, he goes on to deal with every aspect of Godward and manward relationships. No area of our lives is left unclarified. After clarifying man's responsibilities Godward, he deals with interpersonal relationships. He instituted the family and laid down some rules for keeping the family structure inviolate. He created man and insists that man recognize the sanctity of human life. All things were made by him, and he insists on man's right to own and protect property. These are God's requirements for human behavior, and they call for moral decisions on our part.

Society in general is in danger of totally rejecting God's clear standards set forth in the Ten Commandments. The church of Jesus Christ and individual Christians need to stand up and be counted on this matter: God's law is as relevant today as when it was delivered to Moses thousands of years ago. The divine standards of moral behavior are not out of date!

How can I consider myself a Christian and cheat on my income tax? Or betray the sanctity of the marriage bond? Or disregard the principle of the Lord's Day? Or provide a poor example of Christianity to my children and neighbors? The tragedy is that not only has society in general laid the Lord's law in ruins, but so-called Christians are also guilty of rejecting the divine rulebook. That is why society is rapidly disintegrating around us. Everyone has become a law unto himself.

Enforced by the prophets

The moral law of God is important not only because it was enacted by God himself, but also because it was enforced by the prophets. In Matthew 5:17 Jesus links the two: "Do not think that I have come to destroy the Law or the Prophets." Not only was the law enacted by God, but down through Israel's history it had been enforced by the prophets. One after another, they had reiterated God's message, reinforcing it by their teachings and example.

Perhaps what we need today is a visitation from an old-time prophet! Moses, for instance. In Deuteronomy 30:16 Moses said, "I command you today to love the LORD your God, to walk in his ways, and to keep his commands, decrees, and laws." In verse 19 he adds, "I have set before you life and death, blessings and curses. Now choose life, so that you and your children may live." Two words stand out in these verses: *command* and *choose*. They are the essence of the enforcing message of the prophets. God has enunciated moral standards that are his commands, his requirements for living. People must choose whether to obey him or disobey. Jesus did not depart from this standard set forth by God and reinforced by Moses. He supported it!

Look at Isaiah. At the beginning of his prophecy he said, " 'Come now, let us reason together,' says the LORD. 'Though your sins are like scarlet, they shall be as white as snow; though they are red as crimson, they shall be like wool. If you are willing and obedient, you will eat the best from the land; but if you resist and rebel, you will be devoured by the sword.' For the mouth of the LORD has spoken" (1:18-19). Either you are willing and obedient, or you refuse and rebel. Here it is not a communication of command and choice; it is a message of obey or disobey. Have you ever heard someone excuse his way of flaunting the law of God by saying, "I'm not living under law—I'm under grace"? What a travesty on the meaning of grace. Freedom from the law does not mean license to do as I please. It means I now obey God out of love for him, rather than out of fear of his wrath.

Let's look at one other prophet—Malachi.

Ever since the time of your forefathers you have turned away from my decrees and have not kept them. Return to me, and I will return to you," says the LORD Almighty.

"But you ask, 'How are we to return?'

"Will a man rob God? Yet you rob me.

". . . Bring the whole tithe into the storehouse." *(3:7-10)*

God is hitting the people where it hurts. They have broken the first commandment, "You shall have no other gods before me." Also, they have operated contrary to his commandment "You shall not steal." God's moral law is simple, and it is broken in every pew of every church in the land. God says we should not covet, but we covet so much that we cannot support the work of God.

We could say the same about the other seven commandments. We break them all in some way. And the prophets are simply reemphasizing what God said when he made his covenant with his people. Through Malachi God is saying, "Either return to me, or you are rejecting my principles." Do we dare answer as did the people of Malachi's day: "It is futile to serve God. What did we gain by carrying out his requirements and going about like mourners before the LORD Almighty?" (3:14). When we refuse to obey him, that's what we're doing.

Endorsed by Christ

As we look at Jesus in the Bible, we see him in many roles. But I'm afraid we usually fail to see him as the endorser of God's law. He endorsed it by his life in that he totally affirmed its validity: "The one who sent me is with me; he has not left me alone, for I always do what pleases him" (John 8:29). Every day we Christians are faced with opportunities to please the Father. Every time we say no to the temptation to lie, steal, or commit adultery, we are pleasing him. Why do we stand true? Because we love God more than the sin we are tempted to commit. If you want to please the Father as Jesus did, live your life as Jesus did, a total endorsement of the moral law. Notice what he said later in his Sermon: "So in everything, do to others what you would have them do to you, for this sums up *the Law and the Prophets*" (Matt. 7:12, italics mine). We glibly sum up this verse as the "Golden Rule"—but Jesus says the Golden Rule is nothing more or less than the total fulfillment of the Law and the prophets.

Jesus Christ not only totally endorsed the validity and veracity of the moral law by fulfilling it in his life and amplifying it in his teaching; he also acknowledged it by his death. In Galatians 3:13 Paul says, "Christ redeemed us from the curse of the law by becoming a curse for us, for it is written: 'Cursed is everyone who is hung on a tree.' " If you want to know what Christ thought of the law, look at him on the cross. Why did he endure the shame and pain of the cross? Because of the rank immorality and amorality of fallen humanity, who had totally rejected God's law. Jesus Christ was made to be sin for us because of his estimate of that law.

I see the endorsement of Christ on the moral law because it is answered by his Spirit: ". . . that the righteous requirements of the law might be fully met in us, who do not live according to the sinful nature but according to the Spirit" (Rom. 8:4). Do you know that the Bible actually teaches that Jesus endorsed this law so utterly and completely that he affirmed it by his life, amplified it by his teaching, acknowledged it by his death, and answers every demand of the moral law in the life of every person who lives in the fullness of the Holy Spirit?

We speak in hushed tones of living the Spirit-filled life. Do you know what it is? The Spirit-filled life is simply living a life before God and our fellow human beings according to the moral law of a moral God. We may call it the fruit of the Spirit: love, joy, peace, patience, kindness, goodness, faithfulness, gentleness, and self-control, but it means the same thing. God is a unity, and he's saying one thing loud and clear: "I'm a moral being; this is my moral law. You've broken it, but Christ died that you might be forgiven. And he has come to live within you by his Holy Spirit that you might operate according to my stated plan: the total and unequivocal fulfillment of the law." There is no way for us to call ourselves

Spirit-filled Christians if we are not fulfilling the moral law. That's how important it is.

The Permanence of the Moral Law

Jesus spelled out the permanence of the moral law: "I tell you the truth, until heaven and earth disappear, not the smallest letter, not the least stroke of a pen, will by any means disappear from the Law until everything is accomplished" (Matt. 5:18). Jesus was saying that the law is totally and utterly permanent. He prefaced it with "I tell you the truth." This was an authoritative statement, backed up by all that Jesus is.

Not only that, it was also an absolute standard. The theory of relativism is popular in considering behavior today. Fletcher calls it "situation ethics." He makes moral questions relative. What is wrong today may be right tomorrow if the circumstances change. This reminds me of our dilemma with the pornography legislation. Such fuzzy thinking leads into a chaos of confusion. Was Joseph wrong for not giving in to the wiles of the woman who tempted him (Gen. 39:7 ff.)? After all, she was his master's wife, and his job may have depended upon it! No, Joseph did not fall into the trap. He followed and absolute standard: God's law. Not the smallest letter or the least stroke of a pen would disappear in his lifestyle. He chose to obey God rather than do what might have seemed most expedient.

The Relevance of the Moral Law

"Anyone who breaks one of the least of these commandments and teaches others to do the same will be called least in the kingdom of heaven, but whoever practices and teaches these commands will be called great in the kingdom of heaven" (Matt. 5:19). The moral law of God is a principle of behavior for those who are in the kingdom. Jesus says, "If you as a Christian in the kingdom are going to be disobedient in the least area of the moral law, and teach people either by your words or actions that they can deny the moral law with impunity, you will be the least in the kingdom." We have an equation here: Disobedience plus denial equals disgrace. The moral law is relevant to the Christian.

Jesus then goes on to show the results of obedience: "Whoever practices and teaches these commands will be called great in the kingdom of heaven." Here is another equation: Doing plus disseminating equals distinction. We have a choice. Will we be great in the kingdom—or a disgrace? We choose by our attitude toward the moral law of God.

Not only is God's moral law relevant as a principle of Christian behavior; it is also relevant as a prelude to Christian conversion. Jesus makes that clear in Matthew 5:20: "For I tell you that unless your righteousness surpasses that of the Pharisees and teachers of the law, you will certainly not enter the kingdom of heaven." Now he is speaking not to those in the kingdom, but to those still outside. The moral law helps us understand the fallacy of our own self-righteousness. The problem with the Pharisees and teachers of the law, to whom these words were addressed, was this: they were so meticulous in their observance of the letter of the law that they missed the whole spirit of the law. Their attitude meant that they completely lacked the true spirit of worship, for which God longs.

This is what makes the moral law so helpful as a prelude to Christian conversion. It helps me recognize and reject my own self-righteousness; it reveals my unrighteousness. If I break one tiny aspect of God's law, I'm guilty of breaking it all. But the beautiful thing about it is this: When I admit my unrighteousness and my self-righteousness, when I come before God broken in repentance, asking for forgiveness, no matter what my sin is, I'm forgiven. God's law is just, but God is a merciful, loving Judge.

MAKING IT PRACTICAL

1. What is the basis, the source of the moral law? Why did God give it to us?

2. What are some reasons for the moral chaos that surrounds us in society today?

3. In light of the fact that our society today denies the existence of moral absolutes, what is the importance of God's moral law as revealed in the Ten Commandments?

4. How effective is the church in its attempt to stand out against the amorality of society? Why? How could we be more effective?

5. What part does the moral law play in conversion?

6. What are some specific things the individual Christian can do to show how relevant God's moral law is to life today?

For further study, see *The Ten Commandments: God's Rules for Living* by Stuart Briscoe, a Fisherman Bible Studyguide (Shaw).

You have heard that it was said to the people long ago, "Do not murder, and anyone who murders will be subject to judgment." But I tell you that anyone who is angry with his brother will be subject to judgment. Again, anyone who says to his brother, "Raca," is answerable to the Sanhedrin. But anyone who says, "You fool!" will be in danger of the fire of hell.

Therefore, if you are offering your gift at the altar and there remember that your brother has something against you, leave your gift there in front of the altar. First go and be reconciled to your brother; then come and offer your gift.

Settle matters quickly with your adversary who is taking you to court. Do it while you are still with him on the way, or he may hand you over to the judge, and the judge may hand you over to the officer, and you may be thrown into prison. I tell you the truth, you will not get out until you have paid the last penny.

Matthew 5:21-26

8
Anger

So far in the Sermon on the Mount Jesus has been dealing in generalities, but beginning in verse 24 he becomes very specific as he applies the moral law "You shall not murder." The implications of this commandment unfold like a flower before our eyes as he begins to show us the broad intent of this prohibition against murder.

Some Basic Assumptions

At this point in his sermon Jesus assumes that his hearers know the moral law. Ignorance of the law cannot be used by them as an excuse any longer. He states it this way: "You have heard that it was said to the people long ago, 'Do not murder, and anyone who murders will be subject to judgment' " (Matt. 5:21). I think there are two reasons why Jesus could make this assumption.

Knowledge of God's law

First of all, Jewish parents were duty-bound to teach their children the law of God. "These commandments that I give you today are to be upon your hearts. Impress them on your children. Talk about them when you sit at home and when you walk along the road, when you lie down and when you get up. Tie them as symbols on your hands and bind them on your foreheads. Write them on the doorframes of your houses and on your gates" (Deut. 6:6-9). Parents have a moral and spiritual obligation to teach their children God's standard of conduct.

One of the great problems in our country today is simply that parents are not fulfilling their God-given roles. God's blueprint for the home is a program of teaching by the parents, particularly the father, which is to be reinforced by the church, the school, and other areas of influence. Pastors and Sunday school teachers are not supposed to do all the moral teaching. This does not mean that parents provide a desultory prayer occasionally, or a perfunctory "Don't forget your Bible reading" as kids drag themselves from the TV and head for bed. Rather, it means doing the sort of thing that happened as recorded in Nehemiah 8:8, "They read from the Book of the Law of God, making it clear and giving the meaning so that the people could understand what was being read." Notice that not only was the meaning made clear, but the teachers also helped the people to understand what was read.

This is why Jesus assumed that the people knew the moral law, for they should have heard it in their homes and in their churches. Both parents and preachers were to fulfill their obligations.

Respect for God's law

The second assumption that Jesus makes is that the people not only have a knowledge of the law of God, but they also have a respect for it. They believe it, and they believe it in a realistic way. There are three basic reasons why people respect the law of God:

First, they respect it because of its *source*—God himself. If we believe in a Supreme Being (and most people do in one way or another), and we believe that he has given us principles of behavior and operation, for that reason alone we must have unbelievable respect for his law. How can we treat something of divine origin without respect?

Then there is the *scope* of his law. The Ten Commandments touch people in every area of their beings, in every conceivable aspect of their existence. God has spoken to the issues and dealt with the problems that confront us. Nothing is left unsaid.

Finally, we should respect the law because of its *severity*. Not only does God clearly outline his requirements for Christian behavior; he also spells out in no uncertain terms what will happen to the people if they do not play the game according to his rules. God firmly believes in deterrents—that which will frighten a person into acting in a certain way because he realizes what will happen to him if he doesn't. God says, "I am the Lord your God. These are my principles. Do them and you will live. Don't and you will perish." That stimulates respect for the law of God, and Jesus assumed that.

Some Bold Assertions

Jesus makes several assertions that are shattering in their implications. He claims here that his words and the law of God demand equal attention. There are people who make much of the "revealed will of God" and who are deeply impressed by "the law of Moses"—they think these are the bases upon which a civilized society must be built. But they have no time for the sayings of Jesus Christ. Here in Matthew 5:22 Jesus claims equal status: "But I tell you, . . ." There is no question but that the people got the message, for at the end of the sermon (Matt. 7:29) we are told, "He taught as one who had authority, and not as their teachers of the law." The authority with which Jesus Christ spoke made the people sit up and take notice.

What am I trying to say? There are plenty of people who believe implicitly in "You shall not murder," but they do not believe "Anyone who is angry with his brother will be subject to judgment" (Matt. 5:22). They don't believe that anger toward brother is murder—but Jesus says it is! And that's not all.

His second bold assertion is that anger and killing merit equal punishment: "You have heard that it was said to the people long ago, 'Do not murder, and anyone who murders will be subject to judgment.' *But I tell you* that anyone who is angry with his brother will be subject to judgment. Again, anyone who says to his brother, 'Raca,' is answerable to the Sanhedrin. But anyone who says, 'You fool!' will be in danger of the fire of hell" (Matt. 5:21-22, italics added).

The word *judgment* refers to certain crimes for which men could be brought up before the local courts. The next highest court was the Sanhedrin, which met in Jerusalem. Anger is a sin that merits the attention of that tribunal. But even more striking is Jesus' crowning claim: that anger is a sin worthy of the final judgment.

Wait a minute! Did Jesus really say that? Did he say, "If you get mad, you're going to hell"? No, he was speaking figuratively here. He is saying that local judgment, and even higher judgment, and the most severe judgment of all, hell fire, are deserved by the angry man. In this, he was bucking the popular sentiment that excuses anger, glossing it over, making it less serious than it really is. But anger leads to murder, so Jesus was saying, "I take anger so seriously that I believe it is to be weighed in the same balance as murder."

Not only does he point out that anger and killing merit equal punishment, but he proceeds to give us some reasons for this judgment. First of all, anger is murder's root. Look at the murder statistics in our own country and compare them to that of other countries, even places such as Northern Ireland. More people were murdered in the city of Detroit last year than were killed in the whole of Northern Ireland. But here's a striking fact. Most of the murders committed in the United States were committed by one family member against another. Someone lost his temper and went for a gun—murder was the result. That is one reason Jesus comes down so heavily on the subject of anger. It leads to murder. The case of Cain and Abel is a classic example of how a heart filled with anger can erupt into violence against one's brother.

Anger can involve something other than the body, however. It can also destroy an individual's personhood. The word *Raca* in verse 22 means, "You are utterly worthless. I despise you." Later in the verse Jesus uses the expression "You fool," which today would be like saying, "You're stupid." This attitude is destructive of the personhood of the individual at the receiving end of the judgment. Downgrading a fellow human being, who is made in the image of God, is a form of murder, and Jesus condemns this attitude among others in his blanket statement "Anyone who breaks one of the least of these commandments and teaches others to do the same will be called least in the kingdom of heaven" (Matt. 5:19). This applies to Christians, who have known the forgiveness of God, just as appropriately as it applies to the non-Christian. Who is the least in the kingdom? The person who is a Christian, but in personal relationships does not control his temper, who lashes out with his tongue, intent on reducing another person to nothingness. Anger kills personhood.

Anger also destroys community. According to Romans 13, the whole essence of the law of God is love. There is no way that anger can portray love. Neither adultery nor lying reveal love in any way. Blasphemy certainly reveals anything but love. And one thing Jesus is impressing upon his hearers is this: "If there is anything that will wreck the brotherhood of believers and the personhood of all people, it is anger—which leads to insult, which leads to the destruction of human beings. Watch out for it!"

Here's a paradox, however. In some instances, killing may not be sin. Undeniably, the Old Testament teaches or endorses capital punishment. "Anyone who strikes a man and kills him shall surely be put to death. . . . Anyone who attacks his father or his mother must be put to death. . . . Eye for eye, tooth for tooth, hand for hand, foot for foot, burn for burn, wound for wound, bruise for bruise" (Exod. 21:12, 15, 24-25).

That isn't all. Even anger may not be sin. "In your anger do not sin" (Eph. 4:26). This is another of the bold exceptions Jesus makes. If your anger is self-centered, it is sin. On the other hand, if you don't get angry sometimes for the sake of other people, that can be sin as well. Jesus became angry when other people's rights were violated or when the house of God was desecrated (John 2:16). Nehemiah became angry at the exploitation of the common people by their leaders (5:1-8). In both instances, however, anger developed because of injustice done to others.

Some Big Actions God Expects

First of all, Jesus expects us to *recognize* sin for what it is. We must take note of the causes of anger: "For from within, out of men's hearts, come evil thoughts, sexual immorality, theft, murder, adultery . . ." (Mark 7:21). What causes anger? A sinful heart. Pride also causes anger: "The older brother became angry and refused to go in" (Luke 15:28). In the parable of the Prodigal Son, the older son was jealous of the celebration put on by his father when the prodigal brother returned from his rebellious wandering. His pride was hurt and he refused to participate in the welcome-home party. He was jealous of the recognition given his brother—and the lack of recognition given him. We fail to handle our anger if we fail to recognize it for what it is.

We also need to recognize its characteristics. Did you ever, as a husband, want to get even with your wife? Or did you, as a wife, ever want to get back at your husband? That's the spirit Paul was exposing in Ephesians 4:30-32: "And do not grieve the Holy Spirit of God, with whom you were sealed for the day of redemption. Get rid of all bitterness, rage and anger, brawling and slander, along with every form of malice. Be kind and compassionate to one another, forgiving each other, just as in Christ God forgave you." All these actions are characteristic of one sin: anger. All the reactions Paul calls for in verse 32 are the result of one characteristic in the life: love. Bitterness, wrath, anger, clamor, evil speaking, malice—all these are healed and counteracted by love. All of them grieve the Holy Spirit, but love fulfills his will in our lives.

Then we need to *reject* anger's hold upon our lives. Paul says, "But now you must rid yourselves of all such things as these: anger, rage, malice, slander, and filthy language from your lips. Do not lie to each other, since you have taken off your old self with its practices" (Col. 3:8-9). In other words, Paul is saying, these old deeds of the "old self" have nothing to do with the new nature. Reject them. How? Understand what is wrong and say no to it. Understand what is right and say yes to it. If you become angry, it isn't because you cannot help it. It's because you *want* to get angry.

If you get angry and *stay* angry, it isn't because of the terrible provocation you have suffered; it's because you are being disobedient.

The third big action is *reconciliation*. " 'In your anger, do not sin': Do not let the sun go down while you are still angry" (Eph. 4:26). How do you deal with anger? Daily. The problem has to be resolved before sunset. Recognize it.

Men, if you come to church angry at your wife, leave immediately. Get right with her outside the church. Then come in and bring your gift. That's my practical paraphrase of Matthew 5:23 and Ephesians 4:26. If we were to examine the myriad of marital problems rampant in the church today, we would discover that anger lies at the root—anger shown in bitterness, resentment, and hatred. If these roots had been dealt with on a biblical basis, saying yes to the Spirit of God and no to sin, divorce would not have reached such epidemic proportions in the church as it has. If reconciliation had been sought before the going down of the sun every day, the breakdown of "Christian" marriages would not have happened.

We don't solve the problem by looking at the provocation and excusing the anger; we solve it by looking deep within ourselves, at our own sinful heart, and dealing with what we see there. Anger is one of the most common sins overcoming the Christian. We must give our anger to the Lord and let his Spirit fill our lives.

MAKING IT PRACTICAL

1. In the church of God today, how do our knowledge of and respect for God's law compare with the knowledge and respect that Christ assumed his hearers had?

2. How is anger related to murder? How does anger kill personhood? How does it kill community?

3. How is downgrading a fellow human being, made in the image of God, a form of murder?

4. What causes most of our anger? When is this anger not a sin?

5. What are some practical ways that we can counteract the powerful effect that anger can sometimes have in our lives? How can we get rid of our anger? How can we control it?

You have heard that it was said, "Do not commit adultery." But I tell you that anyone who looks at a woman lustfully has already committed adultery with her in his heart. If your right eye causes you to sin, gouge it out and throw it away. It is better for you to lose one part of your body than for your whole body to be thrown into hell. And if your right hand causes you to sin, cut it off and throw it away. It is better for you to lose one part of your body than for your whole body to go into hell.

Matthew 5:27-30

9
Sex

It is vitally important that Christians understand sex as a dynamic, driving force of human life. In our modern day this God-given gift is abused rather than used as God planned it. Terrible sin, degradation, and unbelievable problems riddle our world because of this misuse. The power of anger and the power of sex are two of the most dynamic forces operative in human experience. Christians especially must not only know how to cope with anger; they must also know how to handle sex. Their positive example in dealing with these two forces is vitally important if our Christian witness is to be effective in the world. A godly example is desperately needed. In this chapter we will be looking at some biblical teachings on sex, some alternative theories about sex, and Jesus' teachings in particular on the subject.

Biblical Teachings on Sex

Let us look closely at some passages that offer a biblical understanding of sexuality.

Sex is a fact of life

When I speak of the facts of life, I am not referring to those often embarrassing exchanges between father and son and mother and daughter at the onset of puberty and its mysteries. I am referring to the fact that sexuality is a *divine creation*, planned by God for the human race he instituted: "So God created man in his own image, in the image of God he created him; male and female he created them" (Gen. 1:27). Notice that the differences in human sexuality were part of God's divine plan. This is not a subject for embarrassment or "under-the-counter" exploitation. It's an exalted area of life when used in line with God's stated rules.

Not only is sexuality a divine creation, but also sexual activity is a *divine command:* "God blessed them and said to them, 'Be fruitful and increase in number; fill the earth and subdue it' " (Gen. 1:28). I realize this approach to the subject is not typical of what happens in many church circles today, where sex education is relegated to the schoolyard or the secular schoolroom. Both media are generally condemned by Christians for giving a false perspective and emphasis. But unfortunately the church either treats the subject with benign respect or takes a negative view of this area about which God is very positive and clear-cut. The Bible offers us a solid, sane understanding and a healthy appreciation of sex, if we will only search it out and apply it.

Another thing we should notice—sexual activity is a *divine concern:* "The LORD God said, 'It is not good for the man to be alone. I will make a helper suitable for him" (Gen. 2:18). So important and vital is the union between man and woman that God goes on to say: "For this reason a man will leave his father and mother and be united to his wife, and they will become one flesh" (Gen. 2:24). What is God saying? "Adam, you should not be alone. You need someone with whom to share your life. I will give you a woman to complete you—a companion and a helper." And the strange term "one flesh" refers, among other things, to the physical side of the marriage relationship. It really concerns God when two people come together in marriage but have an unhealthy sexual relationship. It also concerns him when two people have a sexual life outside the marriage bond, for that is contrary to his will. There is no question about it: According to the Bible sex is a fact of life.

Sex is a facet of love

Facet is a lovely word used to describe one of the surfaces of a cut gem. For example, a diamond has many such surfaces, enhancing its beauty and luster. Love, too, has many facets, and sex is just one of them. Our problem in society today is that we have tended to make sex and love synonymous, confusing the two, putting the idea of love in the wrong perspective.

In Greek thought, love is represented by three different words: *agape, philia,* and *eros.* The first word is used to describe God's love, a love that is supposed to operate in the Christian's life because he or she is indwelt by the Holy Spirit. This is the kind of love that sent the Savior to the cross. It is to so permeate the Christian's life that it overflows upon all those with whom we come in contact, regardless of how they in turn treat us.

The second kind of love, *philia,* is a brotherly love, a social kind of love, another facet of love. People who have no sense of the living God within them can and do show this kind of love. They have a concern for people. Often we Christians are put to shame by this kind of love as evidenced in the lives of unbelievers.

There is a third kind of love—*eros.* This is the Greek word from which we get our English word *erotic.* It is not found in the Bible, and it refers to sexual love. You might remember these three kinds of love by thinking of them as sacred (or spiritual), social (or secular), and sexual. The first two kinds of love are to be operative in the life of any Christian, and all three are to be present in the marriage relationship. The needs of two people, man and woman, in all three of these areas are to be met by the "one flesh" marriage relationship. Any union less than this will be less than biblical love, God's best and total plan for humanity.

When two people come to me wanting to marry, one of the first areas I question is their spiritual condition. This usually surprises them, and often they wonder aloud what this has to do with marriage in general and their wedding in particular. My answer to them is summed up in the preceding paragraph. Marriage between Christians implies spiritual unity, social unity, and sexual unity. Anything less is not in accord with God's divine plan. I'm not talking about people who are not united in spiritual love because one became a Christian after they were married. I'm talking about the disunity that exists when a person who claims to know *agape* (spiritual) love marries someone who is dead in that area of life. The Bible forbids it, and I know it just does not work. It is marriage *that falls short of* the biblical model.

I know of other couples whose marriages have broken down because the *philia* aspect of love is absent in their lives. The social dimension is necessary to total marriage. Marriage demands constant adjustment and adaptation, a growing attitude of oneness between maturing people who love each other.

Where does *eros* fit in here? Sexual love is intended to be the very physical demonstration of spiritual love. It is also the underpinning for social love. You cannot divorce any of these aspects of love from the other two. A fullness of love is found in a union of all three. Let me illustrate this truth from the experience of Adam and Eve: "Adam lay with his wife Eve, and she became pregnant and gave birth to Cain. She said, 'With the help of the LORD I have brought forth a man' " (Gen. 4:1). The word translated "lay with" in this context describes the idea of absolute union. The Living Bible uses the term "sexual intercourse" to render this word in our modern terminology. It simply means that in every conceivable area of their lives there was a oneness. They were two human beings, spiritually, socially, and sexually united, who knew each other at every level of their lives, and this knowledge was consummated in one pinnacle experience that crowned the whole glorious relationship.

Contrast their experience with much of what constitutes sexual behavior today. Sex on the purely human level (without the divine dimension) becomes animal behavior because it does not involve getting to know a whole person. It involves getting

94

and having another person's *body,* without knowing that person's inner essence.

The Bible teaches that sex is a force that can get out of control. These basic drives built into us by our Creator can lead to danger if they get out of control. For example, the hunger drive is needed for survival—but out of control it can mean a glutton's death. The same is true of the sex drive. Out of control in the human race, it could lead to chaos. Unlicensed, uncontrolled sexual activity would destroy the human race. This leads us to the control area spelled out by Jesus in the Sermon on the Mount: "You have heard that it was said, 'Do not commit adultery' " (Matt. 5:27). This is God's regulation for handling the potential chaos of uncontrolled sexuality. It is not simply a negative restriction. It is a controlling mechanism for insuring that society will continue to function.

One of our problems in this modern day arises from our rejection of God's demand for the sanctity of sex in the marriage relationship. Adultery and every other kind of sexual sin are running rampant through our world. This leads me to look at three common theories of sexual activity set up as alternatives to the Bible's teachings on the subject.

Alternative Theories about Sex

Three alternative theories are worthy of note here: the Victorian ethic, the playboy ethic, and the permissive ethic. In grouping Victorianism with the other two points of view, I do not mean to imply that the Victorian ethic belongs on the same level. It appears here as an alternative to the biblical view. I do not intend that it be condemned on the same scale of severity. But the Victorian attitude toward sex is as nonbiblical as the other two.

The Victorian ethic

To the Victorian, sex was something shameful, something nice people did not do. Not only was it shameful and naughty; it implied depravity on the part of the participants in the act. Because this attitude makes sexual activity appear sinful, it is anti-biblical.

The Bible says, "Drink water from your own cistern, running water from your own well. Should your springs overflow in the streets, your streams of water in the public squares? Let them be yours alone, never to be shared with strangers. May your fountain be blessed, and may you rejoice in the wife of your youth. A loving doe, a graceful deer—may her breasts satisfy you always, may you ever be captivated by her love" (Prov. 5:15-19).

The Song of Solomon is another glowing description of the beauties and ecstasies of marital love. The Victorian ethic rejects these teachings about sex and in so doing is unbiblical, even anti-biblical in its emphasis.

The playboy ethic

The second alternative is the so-called playboy ethic, which is just the opposite of the Victorian ethic. To the follower of this philosophy, sex is not shameful, it is fun—and the goal is to have as much fun as possible, like kids in a sandbox. No doubt in your town there are "adult" bookstores—but that is a misnomer. Those who frequent such places are not showing maturity but immaturity, people unable to understand sex in its proper perspective.

While the Victorian ethic is anti-biblical, the playboy ethic is anti-social—it results in hedonism, the doctrine that pleasure or happiness is the highest good. Hedonism looks for pleasure to satisfy itself; it is basically selfish and self-seeking. Any person whose thinking is dominated by selfishness will ultimately end up as an antisocial individual, seeking his or her own pleasure at the expense of the well-being of others. This playboy philosophy, if allowed to rule our world, would result in chaos.

The permissive ethic

The reasoning behind the permissive ethic assumes that sex is merely natural, that it is a mistake to restrict what comes naturally.

Human beings are thought to be just like animals in this regard, acting on our natural instincts. To regulate our sex drive is to put unhealthy and unnatural limitations upon us, which will restrict us unduly, creating frustration and needless unhappiness. This is the platform of the permissive ethic. Where does this kind of thinking lead us? It produces what I call perverted alliances.

The first of these is the alliance of *premarital sex*. Sex is meant to be the pinnacle, the consummation of a total relationship: spiritual, social, and sexual. Before marriage there is no way for two people to reach this kind of an in-depth knowledge of one another. Such a relationship demands total commitment, a commitment that cannot exist between people unwilling to commit themselves to the marriage bond.

The second area is the alliance of *extramarital sex*. This is another product of permissive society. The biblical ideal of marriage calls for two people to "leave" and "cleave," forming a new entity by their sexual unity. Any violation of that unity in terms of "extramarital" involvements is a perversion of God's plan and purpose for marriage.

A third perverted alliance is *homosexual*. While the causes of homosexual attraction are hotly debated, there is no doubt that God's standard of sexual behavior is heterosexual, and homosexual behavior is therefore impermissible despite whatever a permissive society decrees. The Bible is clear in its condemnation of this practice. To cite just one passage, "Because of this [their rejection of God], God gave them over to shameful lusts. Even their women exchanged natural relations for unnatural ones. In the same way the men also abandoned natural relations with women and were inflamed with lust for one another. Men committed indecent acts with other men, and received in themselves the due penalty for their perversion" (Rom. 1:26-27).

All these alliances are anti-Christian. In the Bible the family unit is the basic unit in the fabric of society, and these perverted forces are designed to weaken, if not completely destroy, that unit. We need to understand what these alternative approaches to human sexuality are saying.

The Christian Treatment of Sex

Now let's look at the Christian treatment of sex. Believe it or not, the Christian is the only person who can find total delight in the sexual experience that God has planned for his children. Commitment to Jesus Christ and complete enjoyment of sexual joy are not incompatible. The only restriction Jesus places on this relationship between man and woman is that it take place *within the confines of marriage*. Paul tells us, "Each man should have his own wife, and each woman her own husband" (1 Cor. 7:2). Here is a simple statement of fact calling for delight in the sexual relationship within the bonds of marriage.

Notice another aspect of this intimate relationship: it is to be enjoyed *on the level of mutuality.* "The husband should fulfill his marital duty to his wife, and likewise the wife to her husband. The wife's body does not belong to her alone but also to her husband. In the same way, the husband's body does not belong to him alone but also to his wife. Do not deprive each other except by mutual consent and for a time" (1 Cor. 7:3-5). If we are looking for a biblical basis for sex life in marriage, this is it. Sexual fulfillment is in God's design for the marriage relationship.

The second thing Jesus is calling for is *the exercise of sexual discipline* that fulfills the command "You shall not commit adultery." In Matthew 5:28 he says, "But I tell you that anyone who looks at a woman lustfully has already committed adultery with her in his heart." There is such a thing as lust in a look. The experience of sexual delight is biblically valid and necessary, but the exercise of sexual discipline is also biblically necessary. The discipline starts with discernment. Jesus is saying, "Fornication is not just a physical act. It is a mental attitude." Love longs to give, but lust says, "I love me, and I'm going to get this woman for me." I believe this is particularly but not exclusively a problem for men, and that's why I say it this way.

In addition to discipline in this area, we also need to *respect the principle of denial*. Jesus is very explicit on this point: "If your right eye causes you to sin, gouge it out and throw it away. It is better for you to lose one part of your body than for your whole body to be thrown into hell" (Matt. 5:29). What is Jesus saying here? That we should follow his command literally? No, I don't believe so, for where would we stop with this self-mutilation? After the right eye, would the left eye have to go? What about the man who can be turned on by the smell of perfume? Does he cut off his nose? Or the seductive sound of a woman's voice? Does he cut off his ear? Sexual arousal can come from any one of our senses, and Jesus is calling for us to control our senses and *deny* ourselves in all these areas—not to *destroy* our senses. He's not saying we must get rid of every one of our senses, but he *is* saying we must use discernment to understand ourselves, and then use denial as we reject the immoral urge and renounce any illegal actions.

The dynamic for all this is the Holy Spirit. "The fruit of the Spirit is love, joy, peace . . . and self-control" (Gal. 5:22-23). As we write these principles of action deep upon our hearts, we will learn to live by the Spirit in the crucial area of our sexuality.

MAKING IT PRACTICAL

1. What evidence do you see that anger and sex are two of the most powerful forces in human experience?

2. How does marriage involve spiritual, social, and sexual unity? What happens if any one of these areas is out of whack?

3. What is the difference between love and lust?

4. How have the Victorian, the playboy, and the permissive theories about sex affected the church of Jesus Christ? What is the best remedy for such thinking?

5. What do you think about the author's statement that "the Christian is the only person who finds total delight in the sexual experience that God has planned for his children"?

6. What are some specific ways we as Christians, married or not, can affirm God's estimation and expectations of sex?

It has been said, "Anyone who divorces his wife must give her a certificate of divorce." But I tell you that anyone who divorces his wife, except for marital unfaithfulness, causes her to become an adulteress, and anyone who marries the divorced woman commits adultery.

Matthew 5:31-32

10

Divorce

We cannot discuss divorce without dealing further with the whole topic of marriage, the subject of the previous chapter. It is interesting to note that Jesus refused to be trapped into talking about divorce. Rather, he felt that the important thing to talk about was marriage:

Some Pharisees came and tested him by asking, "Is it lawful for a man to divorce his wife?"

"What did Moses command you?" he replied.

They said, "Moses permitted a man to write a certificate of divorce and send her away."

"It was because your hearts were hard that Moses wrote you this law," Jesus replied. "But at the beginning of creation God 'made them male and female.' 'For this reason a man will leave his father and mother and be united to his wife, and the two will become one flesh.' So they are no longer two, but one. Therefore what God has joined together, let man not separate. . . . Anyone who divorces his wife and marries another woman commits adultery against her. And if she divorces her husband and marries another man, she commits adultery." *Mark 10:2-12*

I have found, in my own marriage counseling experience, that often people come to talk about divorce only because they are ignorant about marriage. Our need in today's world is not for a more enlightened approach to divorce, but for a stronger presentation of the biblical principles of marriage. One of our modern society's greatest disaster areas is marital and family breakdown—the disintegration of the family unit. What is needed is an authoritative statement from the Scriptures regarding this all-important aspect of life. The Bible's teaching on the subject of divorce is diametrically opposed to the teachings of society. Secular philosophy and scriptural truth are incompatible, yet in the church today too many of us are secular in our attitude toward divorce.

A Serious Situation

Right in the middle of his discussion of behavior patterns for Christians, the Lord Jesus suddenly launches into a discourse on divorce, indicating something of the seriousness of this problem. Really, it doesn't seem to fit the context of the rest of his teachings. Obviously, his purpose in discussing divorce at this point is to impress upon his hearers the sanctity of the family relationship. They were in extreme danger of absorbing the secular philosophy so prevalent around them.

This secular attitude toward divorce was so liberal that we might almost call it legalized adultery. The abuse of the divorce principle enunciated in the Scriptures is out of the question for the Christian. In re-reading the Scriptures concerning the original institution of marriage, I was impressed with its application, not to Adam and Eve, the first married couple, but to us, their descendants. Genesis 2:24 spells it out for us: "For this reason a man will leave his father and mother and be united to his wife, and they will become one flesh." Adam and Eve had no mother or father, so this statement was not made for their benefit. It sets up the scriptural principle of commitment to one another, which a married couple is to make. Because this is a biblical principle, therefore, "What God has joined together, let man not separate" (Matt. 19:6). These are the words of Jesus, not man's words. And because we ignore their solemnity, the institution of marriage is in serious trouble today, as it was in Jesus' day.

Compare the condition of women in Jesus' day to their condition in the Old Testament: "If a man marries a woman who becomes displeasing to him because he finds something indecent about her, and he writes her a certificate of divorce, gives it to her and sends her from his house . . ." (Deut. 24:1). This is the Old Testament statement of the divorce principle. The woman is chattel: She is nothing but a piece of property, with no rights at all, no better than a slave. For no reason at all, a man could divorce his wife. If she displeased him in any way, this was his way of escape.

The stipulation that something "indecent" must be found in her had gone by the board. The Old Testament required that some sexual misconduct be involved before this action could be allowed, but the Jews had conveniently overlooked that aspect and used this law as an excuse for divorce on any grounds. This was the attitude Jesus was condemning in his statement on the subject.

An escalating problem

Is divorce a problem in the United States? You be the judge. There were 264,000 divorces in the United States in 1940. By 1950 the figure had risen to 385,000. By 1960 it was up to 393,000. The figure for 1970 was 715,000. We have now passed the 1,000,000 mark, though there has been some decline in the 1990s since the peak of the divorce rate in the 1980s. We went from a quarter of a million divorces to more than a million divorces in forty years. And, despite the slight recent decline, there is no indication this trend is being reversed.

Erosion of principles

When I entered the pastorate, the following grounds were admissible for divorce in Wisconsin, U.S.A.: adultery; physical or mental cruelty; incompatibility; desertion; alcoholism; impotency; non-support; insanity; pregnancy at marriage; bigamy; separation or absence; felony conviction or imprisonment; drug addiction; fraud; force or duress; or prior decree of limited divorce. Now the grounds are "no-fault"! But biblically the grounds for divorce are very limited.

This is what Jesus was saying in reminding the people of God's original intent for marriage as announced in Genesis 2 and restated by Jesus in Mark 10:7. "For this reason a man will leave his father and mother and be united to his wife." The first principle is this: *Marriage is a divine principle that is permanent in the eyes of God.* If you disrupt it and interfere with it, you are guilty of going contrary to the Word of God.

Secondly, *marriage is a divine principle that is pleasing to the heart of God.* God's standard statement when his creation was paraded before him was this: "Good." But what did he say when he completed his creation of man and woman? *"Very* good." If there is one concept that thrills God above all others, it is his divine principle of love and marriage—the development of the family unit and all that entails. That is why he made the searching statement that marriage is a divine principle.

Because of this, *divorce is a limited privilege.* Our world has departed from this premise so far that we feel divorce is a constitutional right. Nothing could be further from the truth. Marriage is a divine principle, and the best you can say for divorce is that it is a limited principle. It is a concession to the hardness of heart so evident in Jesus' day and in our own. Those who seek a divorce are refusing to admit their own hardness of heart and desperate need for rescue at the hand of God.

Let me spell it out as simply as I know how. There is a straightforward strictness about God's law. God will accept divorce as a concession to hard hearts when there has been marital unfaithfulness, because the very act of such unfaithfulness is in itself a denial of the bond we Christians profess to have before God. As we discussed in chapter 9, the marriage bond implies a oneness of spiritual, social, and sexual love. If that bond is broken by illicit sexual activity, then the marriage relationship may be broken. It doesn't have to be, however. God is interested in forgiveness, confession, and reconciliation. Marital unfaithfulness is not the unforgivable sin in God's sight, and I'm sure he would rather the offended party would forgive the offender if possible.

An easy procedure

In addition to the escalation of the problem of divorce and the erosion of the principles, there's another development: the easing of the divorce procedure. By this I mean the practice that began in the 1970s and '80s to terminate a marriage without fixing blame on either party. From the humanistic, secular point of view, this is a beautiful, painless solution to a painful process. It saves money, embarrassment, heartache, and harassment. There's even a do-it-yourself divorce kit to allow couples to avoid the hassles altogether.

Have I convinced you that we have a serious situation on our hands? Jesus was convinced of it in his day, and I'm sure he would be more outspoken today.

A Searching Statement

Jesus' statement about these matters in Mark 10 (cited on the first page of this chapter) is given in response to Pharisees who were questioning him. They were testing him; for no matter what he answered, he would offend one of the parties in the crowd by going contrary to their position. Jesus reminded them that Moses' decree was because of "the hardness of their heart," and he returned the discussion to the subject of marriage.

The cause of marital problems is not incompatibility. It is sin and disobedience. The answer to this and other problems facing the church today is not a liberalized approach. It is a return to biblical principles.

It is obvious that all kinds of things can and do go wrong in the marriage relationship. As a result, people can be hurt severely. Like any other pastor, I have been introduced to innumerable heart-rending situations: men who refuse to even speak to their wives for weeks; wives who flagrantly parade their unfaithfulness before their husbands, taunting them and holding them up to ridicule; wives ashamed to appear in public because of the shoddiness of their clothing and unable to invite people into their homes because of lack of furniture; children tormented by the sight of parents physically beating each other . . . and on and on it goes. These problems may be caused by alcoholism. But one thing is clear—all these abuses can be rectified and all these horrendous situations salvaged if the people concerned will begin to recognize that the root cause is sin, and sin must be confessed and forsaken. But so often the hardness of heart that leads people to such reprehensible behavior precludes them from confession, restitution, forgiveness, and reconciliation. "Hardness of heart" is the problem, and any solution that does not solve this is no solution at all.

A Spiritual Solution

Is there a spiritual solution to this desperate social disaster? I believe there is—in the church of Jesus Christ, among people who enunciate the biblical principles and demonstrate the power of the Spirit of God in their lives.

Expose secular thinking

First of all, the church of Jesus Christ must expose the disaster of secular thinking concerning marriage and divorce. Divorce is not a solution. All it does is create more problems.

We also have a social responsibility to expose the fallacy of secular thinking in this area. Divorce is always the product of a marriage, and marriage is the product of a wedding. Have you ever seen a couple get married with the expressed intention of destroying each other? The ideal should be to grow from the marriage ceremony rather than disintegrate from there. That is why I feel the church, which is responsible for so many weddings, should be preparing people for marriage and should be speaking out against the liberalization of divorce laws.

Show a positive example

Secondly, by our lives and our example, we should be sharing the joy there is in marriage founded and lived upon basic biblical principles of love and unselfishness. This can only be done when our solid homes, families, and marriages are being shared with those in trouble.

Incidentally, let me add here my conviction that Christians also have a vital opportunity to serve divorced people. The church is supposed to minister to those in need, but in this area we have failed miserably. Instead, we have ostracized the divorced person, looked down upon him or her, and turned our backs.

Explode the delusion

The third thing we must do is explode the delusion of the selfish thrill. All around us are those who are looking to extramarital affairs to spice up their lives. We should be showing them the delights of spiritual triumph in the marriage relationship, the joys of growing together in every aspect of our lives together: spiritual, social, and sexual.

Give an alternative

There is an alternative to the hardness of heart that ends up in the divorce court, and Ezekiel points it out for us: "I will give you a new heart and put a new spirit in you; I will remove from you your heart of stone and give you a heart of flesh" (36:26). A soft heart for a hard heart—that is the exchange that will solve the divorce problem.

A young wife came to me several years ago to ask what the Bible taught about divorce. She concluded she had no alternative except to divorce her husband. I pointed out that she *did* have an alternative: the soft heart promised by God through Ezekiel's inspired pen. Divorce is the result of hardened hearts, and it can be overcome by the antidote of the softened heart.

"Where do I get a soft heart?" she asked, and I had the joy of pointing her to Christ.

Some months later her husband came to me and said, "I don't know what's happened to her, but I do know that whatever it is, I want it. She's told me something about a new heart. Can I have one?"

I said, "Let's see if we can get you fitted." God gave him a new heart, and he became a new man. The Spirit of God brought those two back together, and theirs is a happy, productive marriage today.

There is an answer to divorce and to the disintegration of our homes and families—the gospel of Jesus Christ!

MAKING IT PRACTICAL

1. What do you think of the author's statement that "our need in today's world is not for a more enlightened approach to divorce, but for a stronger presentation of the biblical principles of marriage"?

2. As you look around you, what is some evidence you see that divorce is a real problem in our society today? How has society's attitude toward divorce affected the church?

3. What should be the church's attitude toward divorce? What should our attitude be, and how should we act, toward divorced people?

4. How do you respond to the author's statement that "the cause of marital problems is not incompatibility. It is sin and disobedience"?

5. What is the solution and the alternative for the problem of hardness of heart?

6. What are some specific ways the church can expose secular thinking and show a positive example?

Again, you have heard that it was said to the people long ago, "Do not break your oath, but keep the oaths you have made to the Lord." But I tell you, Do not swear at all: either by heaven, for it is God's throne; or by the earth, for it is his footstool; or by Jerusalem, for it is the city of the Great King. And do not swear by your head, for you cannot make even one hair white or black. Simply let your "Yes" be "Yes," and your "No," "No"; anything beyond this comes from the evil one.

Matthew 5:33-37

11

Communication

The people of Jesus' day were great ones for taking oaths. They took very seriously the prohibition in the Ten Commandments about using the Lord's name in vain, so they went to great lengths to avoid this kind of disobedience. In fact, they were so concerned about breaking this law that they went to the other extreme of avoiding the name of Jehovah completely. Only once a year was the name mentioned by the high priest. In their common oaths, they substituted the name of heaven—or earth—or Jerusalem. They even went so far as to say, "I swear by my head." Then, because they were not swearing by the sacred name of Jehovah, they treated their oaths as nonbinding. The result was a nation of people whose oaths meant nothing. They had no integrity; they could not be trusted.

This is exactly the opposite of what Jesus intended the Christian life to be. You and I as Christians are to live our lives differently than those around us. We are to handle the driving forces—anger, sex, and so on—on a totally different basis than the society of which we are a part. Now, Jesus is saying, the same is to be true of our communication. It is not to fall into the same worldly pattern.

If communication was important in Jesus' day, think how much more vital it is in our modern world!

The Power of Communication

"In the beginning was the Word, and the Word was with God, and the Word was God" (John 1:1). The Word is the title given the Lord Jesus. It simply means that he is the communication of the hidden idea of God.

Today the whole area of communication is almost frightening in its power, its potential for evil as well as good. It may be used by good people for good purposes, but it may also be used by evil people for bad purposes. The truth of the message and the integrity of the messenger are the factors that determine whether communication is evil or good.

Communication mobilizes the masses

One of the great powers of communication is its ability to move masses of people. Let us examine two instances of this cited in Scripture. The first is found in Nehemiah 8:1-3:

> All the people assembled as one man in the square before the Water Gate. They told Ezra the scribe to bring out the Book of the Law of Moses, which the LORD had commanded for Israel.
>
> So on the first day of the seventh month Ezra the priest brought the Law before the assembly, which was made up of men and women and all who were able to understand. He read it aloud from daybreak till noon as he faced the square. . . . And all the people listened attentively to the Book of the Law.

Following this mass meeting of Israel to hear the Word of God, the people rallied around to rebuild the city of Jerusalem. This is a beautiful illustration of the power of communication to cause a revival among a people who had wandered far from the place God had planned for them. They rose up and confessed their sin—and the nation began to move toward God and for God once more. This is an example of the power of communication.

Joshua offers another illustration. The children of Israel had been wandering for forty years in the wilderness, and now they were on the brink of the Jordan River, waiting to cross over to the city of Jericho. "Joshua told the people, 'Consecrate yourselves, for tomorrow the LORD will do amazing things among you' " (Josh. 3:5). Joshua shared with the people what God had told him about their taking Jericho, and the next day saw Israel enjoy a thrilling triumph over their enemies.

There is no question about it—communication is a tremendously powerful force. There are examples outside of the Bible to back up this premise. Think of the powerful simplicity of the Gettysburg Address, the short speech made by President Lincoln dedicating the national cemetery at Gettysburg, Pennsylvania. It will continue to live in our memories as long as the world continues, I'm sure.

Or, think about some other great communicators from history. Winston Churchill successfully motivated a nation without sufficient weaponry to stand against the tide of Nazi aggression. I can remember Churchill's speeches and his unsurpassed ability to motivate and mobilize a tired and war-weary people. And a man like Martin Luther King shames me when I see how effectively he communicated to the masses in speeches such as "I have a dream."

The evil that can result from communication is best illustrated by the striking story of Adolph Hitler, the inhuman dictator of Germany whose dark designs plunged the world into World War II and almost annihilated a race. He swept an entire nation behind him by the power of his voice.

You and I communicate just as definitely as do a Lincoln, a Churchill, a King, or a Hitler. We communicate constantly. We have the power to motivate as well. Jesus is telling us to be very careful *how* and *what* we communicate. What have we done with our power?

Communication initiates ideologies

Communication also has the power to initiate ideologies. Jesus himself is a marvelous example of this people-moving power. He changed the course of a nation, the history of an entire people, by the precepts he shared in the Sermon on the Mount. We are still being affected by them to this day.

Another less sacred example is Nikolai (or Vladimir Ilyich) Lenin, a Russian revolutionary leader. Along with Karl Marx he spearheaded the godless philosophy known today as Communism, a mass movement that formerly dominated more than half the world's population. These men and their followers initiated a philosophy whose ultimate effect upon the world is yet to be realized.

What about Martin Luther and his ninety-five theses? When he hammered his statements regarding faith and justification upon the door at Wittenburg, he launched a Reformation in the church whose effects are still being felt centuries later—another classic example of the power of communication to initiate a totally new idealogy.

Communication affects attitudes

Communication has the power to affect attitudes. I believe that Madison Avenue has a greater impact on American society today than the church of Jesus Christ. Advertising, whether we admit it or not, affects us to a frightening extent. I'm firmly convinced that our appetites and our attitudes are affected more by the advertising media than they are by anything emanating from pulpits today.

Not only are we affected by the advertising industry, but we are also moved by local, national, and global politics. When one political party is in power, we are told that one particular problem is the most critical and has reached drastic proportions. This might be the government deficit, healthcare, family disintegration, government corruption, environmental pollution, or some other global problem.

Then the other political party comes to power and we are informed that their predecessors were wrong. Some other issue is, instead, at a crisis point and about to blow up in our faces.

Communication creates crises

Communication also has great power to precipitate and create crises. A certain kind of music, for example, can precipitate a certain mood, a certain attitude. Movies, too, are frighteningly powerful in their ability to transmit either evil or good communication. Some of the recent box office bonanzas indicate how this medium can influence an entire nation, even the world.

Billy Kim, a Korean evangelist, tells a story that thrills me with its implications on this matter of communication. After the war the communists swept down into South Korea from the North. One of the first things they did was to gather a group of Christians into the church building, where they demanded that the leaders deny the Lord. They backed up their demands with torture and threats to the lives of their prisoners. One by one the leaders succumbed. When their torturers handed them the Bible and told them to spit upon it, they did so, until the communists came to one little girl.

Fearlessly she looked at her tormentors and said, "You can hammer me into a pulp. You can beat me into extinction, but I will never deny my Lord!" Then, after turning to the leaders who had fallen to say, "May God have mercy on your souls," she began to sing. What was the result? The crowd with her in the church joined her in singing. She turned the tide of denial that had been begun by the leaders. What did the communists do? They executed the leaders who had denied Christ and set free the girl whose courage had been so clearly communicated.

We wonder why the church in Korea is so powerful, so effective in communicating the gospel. One great factor is that there are many believers who, like that little girl, have the power to communicate their lack of fear, their dedication, and their love for Christ.

The Perversion of Communication

Now we want to look at the ways in which now, as never before, communication has become perverted in its ability to shape and mold the masses. How sophisticated the machinery has become! Communication is often perverted through perjury, profanity, and pretense.

Perjury

What do I mean by perjury? In Matthew 5:33 Jesus quoted the Scripture that said, "Do not break your oath, but keep the oaths you have made to the Lord." Perjury is giving one's word, but then going against it. Watergate is a striking example of perjury.

Brilliant people have gone into court to give the impression of total integrity, that what they are saying is total truth—when in reality they are telling a pack of lies. Most of us don't play in that league. But what about our handling of such things as income tax returns and phone calls? Have you ever told a caller the boss wasn't in when she sat across the desk from you, or have you called in sick when you were perfectly well? That's perjury, too.

I wonder if we really listen to our conversations! How often do we stretch the truth (or just bend it a little)? Exaggeration, thy name is legion! Lying seems to be the great American pastime.

Perjury operates in the spiritual realm as well: "When you make a vow to God, do not delay in fulfilling it. He has no pleasure in fools; fulfill your vow. It is better not to vow than to make a vow and not fulfill it" (Eccl. 5:4-5). What about your marriage vows? Were they taken before people—or before God? What about the promises made to God in the early heat of conversion? Were they fulfilled? What about the perjury we commit when we sing, "O for a thousand tongues to sing my great Redeemer's praise," and then fail to use even the one tongue we have to speak up for him? One of the great problems in the church today is this whole matter of perjury—spiritual perjury. We think we can go back on our word without fear of consequences, even before God. How deluded we are!

Profanity

Another perversion of communication today is summed up in the word *profanity.* "You shall not misuse the name of the LORD your God" is one of the Ten Commandments most familiar—and most often broken. To "misuse" means to treat lightly, to use lightly. How often we hear the name of God used in this way: "For God's sake," "God almighty," and so on. Think of the rash of minced oaths: "Jeez"; "Gosh"; "Golly." Every time we use the name of God for anything less than expressing his supremacy in our lives, we are guilty of breaking this commandment.

We also profane God's creation by the use of expressions like "Good heavens"; "Go to hell"; and so on. Jesus, in the Sermon on the Mount, is telling us to watch our lips, to watch our communication.

Pretense

What about the matter of pretense or hypocrisy? There is no better illustration of this than Ananias and Sapphira in Acts 5. For their make-believe, God struck them down. What was their pretense? "Then Peter said, 'Ananias, how is it that Satan has so filled your heart that you have lied to the Holy Spirit and have kept for yourself some of the money you received for the land?' " (v. 3). These two people *lied.* They *pretended* to be more than they were. Pretense is one more perversion of the precious gift of communication, given to us by God.

The Purity of Communication

Let us end our discussion of communication on a positive note. The best way to clean up our communication system is to examine our motives. Briefly they are these: fear and love. If I fear God, if I realize that I must give an account before him for every idle word, I will watch what communication passes through my life and lips. If I have God's love in my heart for people, I'll be careful how I communicate to them. The last thing I will want to do is give them a false impression by profanity or pretense.

Purity of motive

Purity of motive calls each one of us to examine ourselves. Not only must my motives be pure, but as a Christian, I must be transparent in my criticism of those who are guilty of profanity and pretense. We Christians must take our stand as did the little girl in the Korean church. Stand up and be counted! Don't deny God by quietly standing by when his name is belittled.

Purity of method

Purity of method is vital if we are to clean up our communication. We must check Psalm 51 to examine our actions and evaluate our commitment. "Create in me a pure heart, O God, and renew a steadfast spirit within me," we must pray with David (v. 10). We must use James 3 to evaluate and eradicate any inconsistency in our lives that will hinder God's working through us to minister to others.

Communication is the name of the game. What does my life communicate—life and love, or death and hate? May I move the masses with whom I communicate toward the Savior—not away from him!

MAKING IT PRACTICAL

1. What are some of the powerful things that effective communication can accomplish?

2. As communication becomes more global in scope, what are the dangers and the problems that we face? What are some of the opportunities?

3. What are some concrete illustrations of how, as the author states, "Madison Avenue is having more effect upon American society today than is the church of Jesus Christ"? How can advertising affect our appetites and attitudes?

4. What is perjury? What are some examples of spiritual perjury?

5. What are some ways that you as an individual plan to take a stand for more honest and pure communication?

You have heard that it was said, "Eye for eye, and tooth for tooth." But I tell you, Do not resist an evil person. If someone strikes you on the right cheek, turn to him the other also. And if someone wants to sue you and take your tunic, let him have your cloak as well. If someone forces you to go one mile, go with him two miles. Give to the one who asks you, and do not turn away from the one who wants to borrow from you.

Matthew 5:38-42

12
Relationships

One of the greatest problems confronting modern society is the failure of its members to relate to one another. Let's examine what Jesus was saying in this passage. First of all, the relationships of which he speaks operate within his kingdom. Unfortunately, we realize that the king of this world is not the Lord Jesus Christ. The Bible teaches that Satan has this old world in his grip. Many of the institutions and organizations in our world today are not the product of the kingship of Jesus Christ. He is not the author of our problems. These are the products of the kingship of Satan. This is why we sometimes encounter problems. As Christians we are members of the kingdom of God, but as human beings we must live in a world dominated by Satan. Thus we are constantly confronted with conflict: How does a member of the kingdom of God function in a society manipulated not by the God whom he or she worships, but by a ruler in total opposition to him? That is the crux of the Christian's constant conflict. It is important that we understand this, because as we look at some of the issues that Jesus Christ speaks to here, we would run into some terrible problems if we tried to put them into operation in some of the secular areas in which we're required to work and live.

How should we apply the statement in verse 39, "Do not resist an evil person"? Some believers feel very strongly that this command applies to the nations of the world. A significant segment of the church feels that this principle, if built into international relations, would produce world peace. But to achieve that glorious end requires nothing less than the agreement of all parties—not a very promising prospect! Is it likely that Hitler would have been stopped by the turned cheeks of a million Jews?

We must be careful, however, not to go to the other extreme. Many people have chosen to ignore the principles entirely. This attitude cannot be right, because Christ never taught in order that he might be ignored! I believe in this passage there are principles that we can neither ignore—nor can we impose them on a godless world. Rather, we must apply them as Christians in our lifestyle as members of the kingdom of God on earth.

Relationship Potential

John Donne wrote, "No man is an island." Isolationism is impossible. No human being can be totally self-sufficient and thoroughly self-contained. For very obvious reasons, we are all members of society, and because we are, we're interrelated and interdependent. We are relational beings. The relationships we build have tremendous potential for development, or they have terrible possibilities for destruction. The right kind of relationship can bring about great growth, a beautiful expansion of personality—and the wrong kind of relationship can create chaos, the literal destruction of personhood.

Scripture is full of illustrations of healthy, helpful relationships. Look at an unlikely pair like Paul and Barnabas. Remember how suspicious the early church people were of the newly converted Paul? Only Barnabas welcomed him with open arms, and God worked miracles through that relationship. Saul of Tarsus had been a hothead, a persecutor of the Christians. Barnabas was known as a great encourager. What a beautiful person he must have been. As a result of these two totally *different* people being brought together, the church gained a whole new vision of its place in God's plan and program. Barnabas was the supporter; Paul, the initiator, the spokesman.

As Christians, every one of us needs relationships. We need people with whom we can unburden ourselves, with whom we can simply *be* ourselves. It is vitally important that you and I as Christians be involved in relationships that build up people in every dimension.

As I think back upon my own life, I remember with gratitude certain people who had a tremendous influence upon me. First of all, my parents left their mark upon me, shaping my early life. In the business world, several outstanding men had their effect upon me. I remember my immediate superior in the bank where I first worked. What a disciplinarian he was! As a young bank teller, I had great fear of that man, for he insisted that my accounts must balance every night before I could go home. But the discipline and determination in his life were growing experiences for me. Later on, there were many great men of God whose lives influenced mine in the ministry.

You and I are relational people. We are either expanded or constricted by those with whom we go through life. And of course we have a similar impact on them. Are we encouragers like Barnabas? Or do we destroy those closest to us? Unfortunately, there are people whose aim seems to be to rip others apart. Sometimes even husbands and wives reach this kind of an impasse in the marriage relationship—or parents and children seem intent upon destructive rather than constructive relationships. People within the same church fellowship can get into this kind of situation as well.

These destructive relationships result in the destruction of people with whom we should be building positive ties. If you or I have ever had such a negative or destructive relationship with another person, that breach must be healed and the rebuilding process must begin. We must first of all ask God for forgiveness, and then go to the person we have wronged and ask for his forgiveness.

Relationship Pollution

We live in a nation built on the conviction that people have certain inalienable rights. This premise in itself leads to conflict. Somewhere along the way your inalienable rights and mine are going to come into conflict or confrontation. I realize that I may sound unpatriotic and un-American, but the fact remains that this "great American philosophy" can lead to a fragmented society.

Think of the potential problem in the marriage relationship if both partners insist upon their rights. Such a concern for human rights can lead a man into pretty direct conflict with his wife. And the same is true in any business relationships we might discuss.

The right to dignity

Have you ever worked with someone who insisted on his or her right to be treated with dignity? That person is so prickly that only a select few can associate with him or her. This is the kind of person who would question Jesus' statement in verse 39: "If someone strikes you on the right cheek, turn to him the other also." Such a person would, rather than turn the other cheek, retort, "After all, I have my rights," and lash back.

The right to security

Beside those who say, "Don't insult my dignity," there are those who insist, "Don't interfere with my security." These are the people to whom Jesus was speaking in verse 40: "And if someone wants to sue you and take your tunic, let him have your cloak as well." What is the normal reaction when one is faced with a suit like this? Hire the best attorney you can find. But Jesus was literally suggesting that his Jewish family (and those of us who claim to be his spiritual family) give up not only our garments but even our "security blanket" (The cloak was used by the Jews as a blanket at night) rather than risk severing a relationship. That was a revolutionary idea in his day, and in ours as well. One of our inalienable rights, we feel, is the right to our own security. This lies behind our idea that we have the right to carry arms to protect our homes and loved ones, to make ourselves secure. What carnage could result if this philosophy were allowed full sway in our society, if we were at full liberty to insist on our own rights. I have a right to dignity and security, but if I insist too strongly on these rights, I may end up with no one with whom I can have a relationship!

The right to privacy

Jesus dealt with another of these "inalienable" rights: the right to privacy. "If someone forces you to go one mile, go with him two miles" (v. 41). You will remember Jesus was speaking to a group of people at the complete mercy of the Roman soldiery. It was quite common for these rough Roman soldiers to use Jews as their beasts of burden—to compel them to carry their loads. A good example of this is Simon of Cyrene, who was compelled to carry Jesus' cross. It wasn't his idea. He was drafted. Suppose you had tickets to a ball game this evening, but your boss wanted you to work overtime. That would be an invasion of your privacy! And you'd be reluctant to let it happen. Insisting on your rights might not have the desired effect upon your relationship with your boss—but gladly surrendering your right to privacy would be a different story!

The right to property

In verse 42 Jesus dealt with another right: "Give to the one who asks you, and do not turn away from the one who wants to borrow from you." Now he is touching on our basic right to preserve our own property. Our natural instinct is to protect our own property, but Jesus is telling us to give up that right in this remarkable command.

What was Jesus saying? In modern terminology, I believe he said, "If you want to pollute a relationship, here's how you do it: Insist on no one insulting your dignity. Make sure no one interferes with your security. Protect your privacy at all costs. And don't let anyone infringe on your property rights." These four areas are at the root of most of our societal problems today.

Another way to pollute a relationship is the practice of reaction. In every area so far discussed, Jesus was looking at the possibility of reaction—normal reaction. What's the normal reaction when someone strikes you? To strike back. That's how and why wars are fought. Reaction is automatic. But what does it do to relationships? It shatters them.

What is Jesus suggesting? The Hebrew law allowed "eye for eye, and tooth for tooth." That was a limitation the law laid down. People seem to interpret this as "getting even" whenever you are wronged. It was not so much a mandate to get his tooth as he got yours—but rather an insistence that if you must react to his action, your reaction must be no greater than his action. It is a limitation. No more than one tooth for one tooth! But Jesus is urging something different. He says, "Don't simply work within your legal right. Don't work within the permissible limits of retaliation. Rather, go in the opposite direction. Don't resist the evil that comes to you personally." Admittedly, this is difficult. Our natural inclination is to protect ourselves, to retaliate if we are wronged.

What happens when this urge to react is running rampant within a marriage? There are two people under one roof both insisting on *their* rights. There is total opposition to one another. Can you call that marriage? In the business world if management and labor both insist on their rights, what do you have? A strike. This insistence on one's rights and the accompanying lust for retaliation will break down relationships every time. To counteract this natural tendency to shatter rather than build, Jesus offers us several suggestions.

Relationship Principles

Jesus offered us several principles that act as oil in the relationship machine. By following these we will find more godly relationships that benefit everyone.

Turn the other cheek

Do we take this literally? This reminds me of the old Irish preacher who had been a boxer. He came to a certain city where he intended to hold meetings. As he was setting up his tent, some local toughs came up to heckle him. They had decided to run him out of town. One of them took a swing at the preacher and hit him solidly on the right cheek, knocking him to the ground.

People who knew that the preacher had been a professional boxer expected him to come up swinging, but he didn't. Instead, he got back to his feet, rubbing the right side of his jaw. To the amazement of those who knew, he walked up to the man who had hit him. Indicating his left cheek, he invited the man to hit him again, which he did.

Slowly the ex-boxer rose to his feet, carefully took off his jacket, and rolled up his sleeves. Then he clenched his fists saying, "The Lord gave me no further instructions." *Smack!* (I think he missed the point.)

If we want to know what Jesus meant when he said to turn the other cheek, look at his own example. What did he do when someone struck him on the cheek at his trial? Did he say, "Here, now hit me on the other side"? No, in most instances such an action would be provocative. Or such an attitude may be little more than a display of "intestinal fortitude," showing courage in the face of pain. Instead, Jesus is saying, "If they are after your dignity, let them have it. If they want your security, give that to them as well."

Paul wasn't as good at turning the other cheek as Jesus was. Do you remember what happened when Jesus was on trial? At his trial,

Jesus "made no reply" (Matt. 27:14). How did Paul react? He called the high priest Ananias a "whitewashed wall" (Acts 23:3). Paul had his problems with this principle of nonretaliation expressed by Jesus.

Put yourself in the other person's shoes

If someone strikes me on the cheek, my immediate reaction is to strike back, but Jesus says I am to look at this situation from the other person's point of view. What is *his* problem? Have I done something to precipitate this situation? It would be better for me to examine the whole matter keeping a cool head, hoping to build a bridge rather than tear down a relationship completely. This works in the home between wife and husband, parents and children. It works in the office between employees and employer. If we can just stand back from the situation and seek to understand it, we may be in a position to repair the breach rather than widen it. We stand a chance not only of maintaining a relationship, but also of strengthening it.

Concentrate on your responsibility

In any relationship, if I insist on my rights as a primary consideration, I immediately jeopardize my chances of maintaining that relationship or building upon it. This is true in the home between husband and wife or parents and children, in the office between employees and employer. If my first consideration is my own rights in any given situation, I will doom the relationship at the outset. If my first concern is the other person, I can then begin to build and deepen the relationship we already have. Concentrate on your responsibilities, and the other person's "rights" will be met. This should lead him to responsibility in his treatment of you—and thus your rights will be met.

Let the Holy Spirit guide your responses

If someone strikes me on one cheek, I am to turn to him the other. Do you know what that would demonstrate? Self-control, one of that cluster of fruit listed by Paul in Galatians 5:22-23. Related to that virtue is the quality of self-denial. If a man demands my coat, I will give him my blanket (cloak) also. If someone makes me go with one mile, and I go the second mile, that's a demonstration of self-sacrifice.

These principles sum up what the Christian life is all about. The normal Christian life is the rejection of accepted secular standards of behavior and replacing it with behavior that is enlivened by the Holy Spirit. If my life is lived under control, the working of his Spirit will be evident in my life. Instead of *reacting* blindly to any provocation, I will *respond* lovingly. When I say no to my own rights and yes to God, I am responding as a Christian. What happens when I respond instead of react? I begin to build bridges and relationships, instead of tearing down and destroying them. Remember—God has promised to enable each one of us as Christians to live this kind of life.

MAKING IT PRACTICAL

1. Think of some of the relationships in which you are involved, focusing on the impact each person has on you, as well as your influence on them. What seems to be the key, in your opinion, to having positive relationships?

2. The author says, "We are either expanded or constricted by those with whom we go through life." As you think through some of your relationships, how have you found this to be true?

3. What are some specific ways we can encourage other believers and build them up? What relationships are you involved in where you have the opportunity to help people meet their objectives, grow, and develop?

4. What is the danger of focusing on our "inalienable rights"? In this passage, how does Jesus deal with the idea of our rights?

5. If you have been involved in a negative or destructive relationship with another believer, such as the author describes, what are some ways the breach might be healed and the rebuilding process begun?

You have heard that it was said, "Love your neighbor and hate your enemy." But I tell you: Love your enemies and pray for those who persecute you, that you may be sons of your Father in heaven. He causes his sun to rise on the evil and the good, and sends rain on the righteous and the unrighteous. If you love those who love you, what reward will you get? Are not even the tax collectors doing that? And if you greet only your brothers, what are you doing more than others? Do not even pagans do that? Be perfect, therefore, as your heavenly Father is perfect.

Matthew 5:43-48

13
Love

Love is one of the most talked about and least understood subjects in our society today. I'm convinced that the reason our world is in such difficulty can be traced to this basic misunderstanding of what love is all about. Apparently this was true in Jesus' day as well, for he devoted one whole section of his Sermon on the Mount to the subject.

Christian love is totally different from the world's concept of love. It is unique. In the Sermon on the Mount, Jesus addressed himself to many of the great motivational forces at work in our society. Since love is one of the greatest motivational forces, it is not surprising that he devoted so much attention to it. Without God's kind of love, of which Jesus was the human expression, our world is headed down a path of no return. Unquestionably, society's problems can be traced to a misconception of the meaning of love.

The Magnificence of God's Love

The measure of God's love is impossible to gauge with human instruments. In Matthew 5:45 Jesus said, "He causes his sun to rise on the evil and the good, and sends rain on the righteous and the unrighteous." What does that have to do with love? Look at verse 48: "Be perfect, therefore, as your heavenly Father is perfect." We could substitute the word *mature* here for *perfect,* which is closer to what Jesus is saying. He's not talking about sinless perfection—he's talking about love, about kindness, about a maturity in God that is broader than mere language can convey. Unbelievable as it may seem, the magnificence of God's love is intended to be worked out in the lives of God's children.

God's love reflects his nature

There is such a thing as family likeness. How common it is for us to say that a son is the "image of his father" and a daughter is "as lovely as her mother." Our human minds sometimes find it difficult, if not impossible, to grasp the implications of human likeness, but how much more mind-boggling is this matter of divine likeness. We are to be like our heavenly Father—that's what Jesus is saying here. And one of the most striking ways we can show this likeness is through sharing the love of God.

When people think of a God of love, they often misconstrue this to mean an insipid, sickly kind of love. They think of God as someone who wants and needs love. This concept couldn't be farther from the truth. By his very nature, God is love. He didn't create man because he *needs* love; he created him because he *is* love.

In a sense, this truth is what Jesus pointed out when he reminded his hearers that God made the sun and causes it to shine on everyone. He made everything, but the sun is one of the most beautiful things he made, as we contemplate its meaning to our world. He not only made it; he shares it with us. If he didn't, where would this world be? Whose sun is it? *His* sun, says Jesus. That's the essence of his love.

What does that mean for me? If I'm to represent him here, I must share that love, too. There is no such thing as selfish, me-first love. Love by its very nature must share.

Not only does he *share* his love, he also *sends* it. Notice the next phrase in the verse, "and sends rain on the righteous and the unrighteous." "For God so loved the world that he gave his one and only Son, that whoever believes in him shall not perish but have eternal life" (John 3:16). No one verse better epitomizes the full-orbed meaning of God's love than this brief, beloved sentence. As he talks to his audience on the Mount, Jesus is saying in essence, "If you want to do anything in the world, if you are going to make any kind of a meaningful impact, then you must understand this: You are going to have to be children of your Father, reflecting his nature—and his nature is *giving* love."

God's love meets our need

The magnificence of God's love is not only according to God's nature; it is also according to man's need. God has tremendous resources—the sun and the rain are just a part of his creation. And he is ready and waiting to share those resources. Look around us today. Who is taking credit for the energy resources surrounding us? Humans. Who is messing things up? Humans. Who's really in control? God. "The earth is the LORD's and everything in it" (Ps. 24:1). Everything in it—all the oil, coal, and all the other forms of energy we call ours.

God loves according to need, not according to character. The sun and the rain are available to the evil and the good. How thankful we should be for that fact! If our goodness determined the measure of his blessing, how impoverished we would be. If it was up to us to apportion out the rain and sun, only a select few would enjoy such benefits. But that's not the way of God's love. Human love responds to a character of which we approve. God's love comes *in spite* of character, not *because* of.

The Mediocrity of Human Love

In contrast to God's love, the first thing about human love that makes it mediocre is that man reserves the right to hate. We've looked at our human rights before in this book, and as you recall, insistence upon one's rights is what breaks down relationships. As human beings, we feel we have an inalienable right to reject certain people. This is why we know so little about the love of God. The love of God doesn't hate people—it hates what they do.

How many of us are guilty of wishing evil upon another person? Two of us are in line for a job. The other person falls and breaks his leg, so I get the position. Do I feel sorry—or secretly glad about my good fortune and his misfortune? Or consider one who seems to have everything life could offer—and then loses it. Am I genuinely sorry for him, or secretly glad that he's down where I live now? Human love reserves the right to wish evil upon another, but divine love never does.

"Love your enemies and pray for those who persecute you." How foreign such actions are to the human spirit. That's why we need an injection of the Holy Spirit! In Jesus' day as now, people insisted upon their rights to hate, to reject those who "persecute us." But Jesus calls us to melt our hard hearts, our frozen attitudes, and begin to react in love.

Peter touched on this in his first Epistle: "Keeping a clear conscience, so that those who speak maliciously against your good behavior in Christ may be ashamed of their slander" (1 Pet. 3:16). This is what it means to "persecute" another person. If you and I want others to believe we are children of our heavenly Father, we must be above such behavior, even though the world around us indulges in it.

"Those who persecute" are those who apply pressure, who grind others into the dirt if they get the chance. Of all people, Christians are not to be guilty of that kind of conduct. The fact that we can slip into it at a moment's notice is the reason human love is so mediocre. If you are going to be God's person, you cannot settle for mediocre love—you must insist on magnificent love.

One of the most telling criticisms of the church today is our lack of love for those unlike us. Christian love doesn't only extend to those just like me. It is supposed to extend to all men! The watching world looks at the church and sees how we "love one another"—but they fail to see much evidence of our love for those outside the church. Because we restrict our love to certain attitudes, special occasions, and limited activities, we show only a mediocre human love instead of a mature Christian love.

The Maturity of Christian Love

In contrast to human love, God's love comes from him, is manifested in action, and is a command.

Love is a command

What does God demand of the Christian? " 'Love the Lord your God with all your heart and with all your soul and with all your strength and with all your mind'; and, 'Love your neighbor as yourself' " (Luke 10:27). First and foremost, we are to love God—emotionally (with all our heart and soul), intellectually (with all our mind), and physically (with all our strength). That pretty well touches on every area, doesn't it?

The second major demand is that we love our neighbors as ourselves. Have we ever realized that God loves other people as much as he loves us? It came home to me one day that God had made a world full of unique individuals, and he loved every one of them just as much as he loved me. I am only one among millions.

What am I trying to say? It's perfectly biblical to love myself and consider myself unique and special. But I am not to be self-centered and selfish. I also have the responsibility to realize that other people are special, too. I am to love them as much as I love myself. God has given me a certain sphere of influence and a certain set of gifts, and I am to function in that sphere and use those gifts for others.

His demands are simply this: "Love me and love your neighbor, in that order." Not only that—the uniqueness of the Christian position is that I'm to love my enemy, too!

Do you know what is going to happen to our world? If there is not a revival of the church of Jesus Christ that begins to produce men and women who really love with this all-consuming love of God, society is going to disintegrate. Love God, yourself, and others (including your enemies). That's the divine demand.

Love is shown by action

We are also called upon to display our love. How do I display my love for God? By my obedience to his commands. How do I show my love to others? Read the story of the Good Samaritan. Who is my neighbor? The man in the ditch whose body has been battered, whose life has been almost snuffed out by robbers, the man who *needs* me. If I ignore him as did the Levite and the priest, how am I different from the rest of the world? But if I minister to his needs as I would to my own, then I am showing divine love. How do I show this love? By sacrifice. It's not an easy kind of love.

How do I show love to those who hate me, who misuse me? By the way I respond to them. That's not easy, either.

Love comes from God

Where does this kind of love come from? Do I whip it up in myself? Does it come from within me? The force of Christian love comes from God's powerful *example*. Let me illustrate what I mean.

Years ago the four-minute mile was considered humanly impossible. Runners had been running for years, but no one had ever broken the magic barrier of four minutes. Then Roger Bannister of England broke the barrier. He ran the mile in less than four minutes. Do you know what happened? Since Roger Bannister ran that mile in four minutes, many, many others have done it. Why have so many done in recent years what no man had done in previous years? Among other reasons, they saw that it could be done because Bannister did it. The power of example.

Love also comes from the power of his *expectation*. What does God expect of us? "If you greet only your brothers, what are you doing more than others? Do not even pagans do that?" (v. 47). It's a great thing to suddenly discover the divine expectation. I'm a preacher today because I suddenly discovered that it was expected of me. The only reason I ever wrote a book was that I discovered it was expected of me. What tremendous power there is in the divine expectation. Every one of us is faced with this divine expectation.

The power to love comes from my *experience* of God's love. As I experience his love in my life, I am enabled and energized to do his will. As the power of the Spirit of God is working in my life, I am able to carry out what he expects of me. God makes no demands on us that he does not equip us to carry out. I am to love God, myself, others (even my enemies). And I can do it because the example is there, the expectation is there, the experience is there, and the *enabling* is there. If that is true, and it is, then let us get on with business of living lovingly!

MAKING IT PRACTICAL

1. How can some of today's problems be traced to a misunderstanding of the true meaning of love?

2. What are some specific ways God's love is different from human love? How can our love become more like his?

3. What is the difference between selfishness or self-centeredness and a proper kind of self-love?

4. How does Christian love show itself to be different from the the world's kind of love? Where does Christian love come from?

5. How can we actively show our love for God? What are some ways we can actively show our love for others?

Be careful not to do your "acts of righteousness" before men, to be seen by them. If you do, you will have no reward from your father in heaven.

So when you give to the needy, do not announce it with trumpets, as the hypocrites do in the synagogues and on the streets, to be honored by men. I tell you the truth, they have received their reward in full. But when you give to the needy, do not let your left hand know what your right hand is doing, so that your giving may be in secret. Then your Father, who sees what is done in secret, will reward you.

Matthew 6:1-4

14
Charity

As we move into the sixth chapter of Matthew, we enter a new section of the Sermon on the Mount—the portion having to do with religious observances. Among these traditional observances in the Jewish way of life were the giving of alms (or charity), prayer, and fasting. As people tend to do, the "religious" Jews were carrying things to an extreme, as Jesus points out.

This hypocritical show of piety in giving extended to other areas of religious observance as well: prayer and fasting. These people were more interested in making an external impression than an internal observance. They were ostentatious rather than worshipful in their attitudes.

Jesus has some striking and pungent things to say on this matter. Charity, prayer, and fasting are to be integral parts of the Christian life. But as with other aspects of the Christian life they can be perverted. And that is what these people had done.

Unfortunately, they had so confused the issue of giving alms that they thought charity and righteousness were synonymous. In their thinking, those who gave were righteous, and those who were seen to give were accordingly recognized as being righteous!

Because their motives were perverted, these people were more interested in ostentatious performance than they were in an inward reality. They wanted to put on a show without changing on the inside. They wanted their "righteousness" to be on display. But righteousness is something you *are* and *do,* not something you show off like a new car. The problem in Jesus' day was that the ostentatiousness had been accepted as the real thing. In this chapter we will concentrate on the matter of charity, but our findings will apply equally well to being genuine in the areas of prayer and fasting. First of all, we will look at charity as a product of righteousness, then as a real peril in religion, and finally as a promise of reward.

A Result of God's Righteousness in Us

Righteousness can be many different things in the Word of God, but to begin with, righteousness is an attribute of God. God is absolutely righteous. One of the solid foundations upon which we can build our lives is this fact.

Righteousness is discovered

Righteousness is a requirement of God. He expects people to live in line with his demands set forth in the Ten Commandments. This is where humanity has failed him and gone far astray from his original plan and purpose. To reconcile us with himself, God sent his Son, Jesus, to die for our sins, that we might be made right with God—or declared righteous. One is not made righteous by doing kind things for people, giving alms, praying, and fasting. Being made righteous is the result of accepting God's action on our behalf in forgiving sin through the sacrifice of Jesus on the cross. A person who has been made righteous in this way then seeks to act in a righteous way out of the inner resources of his or her relationship to Christ.

To build a straight wall, we need a plumbline—that is our standard. To be righteous, we also need a plumbline, a standard, and that standard is God himself. If I'm going to recognize his righteousness and apply it to my life, then I need to reject my own *self*-righteousness. What is self-righteousness? That's saying to myself, *I'm all right* when God says "You're not all right." My wall is crooked, but I say it's straight. Does that make it straight?

Every one of us has a tendency to revel in our own self-righteousness. We are ready to justify what we do, rather than to reject our self-righteousness and repent of it. But that is what we must do. The Bible says that our righteous acts are like filthy rags (Isa. 64:6). The very best we can come up with, compared with what God wants and expects, is like a filthy rag. But realize this: Once I have rejected my own self-righteousness and repented of it, God is then prepared to give me his righteousness in Christ. He is ready to forgive me and give me a new righteousness. I'm forgiven, restored, reconciled to God. And true charity is a product of that divine righteousness.

Jesus is not condemning any public act of piety. He is simply saying my motive must be right. If I do it to be noticed, to bring glory to myself, then my motivation is wrong. But we must not let this be an excuse to sit around doing nothing, as some people do. They have decided to show their piety and their humility by doing absolutely nothing. That's not the thrust of what Jesus is calling for here. For example, conversion is a very public act. Paul exemplifies that. Paul's conversion was so public that everyone could see it. But his righteousness was properly on display, for notice who received the glory—God. We are to make absolutely certain that when we have discovered righteousness we display it to the glory of God.

Righteousness is displayed

We also need to make a public *confession* of righteousness. Notice what Jesus says in Matthew 10:32-33: "Whoever acknowledges me before men, I will also acknowledge him before my Father in heaven. But whoever disowns me before men, I will disown him before my Father in heaven." No, Jesus does not reject public piety; he is rejecting public hypocrisy, the falsely motivated act that seeks to give glory to the actor rather than God. Personal, private piety is fine—but it has to be public, too, or it will not bring glory to God.

Paul dealt with this truth in Romans 10:9-10: "If you confess with your mouth, 'Jesus is Lord,' and believe in your heart that God raised him from the dead, you will be saved. For it is with your heart that you believe and are justified, and it is with your mouth that you confess and are saved." Later on in this same chapter, Paul points out the spread of the gospel is a chain reaction set off by public confession of Christ: "For, 'Everyone who calls on the name of the Lord will be saved.' How, then, can they call on the one they have not believed in? And how can they believe in the one of whom they have not heard? And how can they hear without someone preaching to them?" (vv. 13-14). Righteousness, when it is discovered, must be displayed.

One further area where we display our righteousness is in the sacrament of the Lord's Supper, the taking of *Communion.* What a personal, private act of worship this is or should be—but it is to be a public act as well. Paul again points out: "For whenever you eat this bread and drink this cup, you proclaim the Lord's death until he comes (1 Cor. 11:26). That word *proclaim* is better translated "declared" or "preached." Whether we realize it or not, every one of us is a preacher when we take Communion.

Riighteousness is also displayed through *charity.* Charity was very necessary in Jesus' day, as it is today. There were people who were destitute, completely dependent on the charity of others. If you travel in the Middle East today, you will find abject poverty, despite the oil-rich sheiks in the higher echelons of society. Beggars abound today as they did in Jesus' day. Christians have a responsibility in this area of life as well. One of the areas where we show our righteousness is in this matter of concern for the impoverished and underprivileged. How many people have seen our righteousness on display in this area? True, we are not to do charitable things "to be seen by [men]." But Jesus doesn't follow this with an "if." In Matthew 6:2 he says, *"When* you give to the needy . . . ." In verse 3 he again says, *"When* you give . . . ." Our Lord expects his followers to give of themselves and their means to those who are really in need.

Remember what was pointed out earlier in the chapter on "Light of the World"? We are to let our light shine. Notice again the motivation spelled out in Matthew 5:16, "that they may see your good deeds and praise your Father in heaven." Those who give to the needy to be praised by people have their reward. The child of God operates in a different dimension. Before charity comes conversion, confession, and communion—in that order. When that happens, the Father gets the glory, not the child.

Righteousness is disciplined

In addition to being discovered and displayed, our righteousness should be disciplined. One obvious reason for this is that charity can be summarily abused. Charitable acts are not a means of earning salvation; they are evidence of our salvation. One reason the church is not as effective as it might be in spreading the good news of salvation is this: Some Christians are more interested in building big bank accounts, driving big cars, and living in big houses than they are in obeying Christ's admonition to display their righteousness by acts of charity. Many outside the church are more charitable than those in the church. This is where discipline must come in.

Charity is more than dropping a dime in someone's tin cup. It's more than a quarter in the Salvation Army basket at Christmas time. It is an *aware*ness of the needs of others and a giving spirit that is a product of a right relationship with God.

More than awareness, however, there is a discipline of being *active*. Too many of us are like a perfectly tuned car with its engine idling smoothly. Someone needs to climb in and put the car in gear! What does it take to get our wheels moving? All it takes is obedience, and we've already touched on that area in a previous chapter. The priest and the Levite in the story of the Good Samaritan were certainly *aware* of the man in the ditch, but the Samaritan was the only one who put wheels on his awareness and did something about the man's need. After awareness there must come activity.

But after awareness and activity, there must come a willingness to be *alone*. In Matthew 6:3-4 Jesus said, "When you give to the needy, do not let your left hand know what your right hand is doing, so that your giving may be in secret." Jesus is using a figurative expression here to impress upon us that what we do must be done to the glory of God. This calls for the discipline of being alone before God in this matter of charity.

The Peril of Religion

Do you remember the introduction Jesus gave to his parable of the two men who went up to the temple to pray? "To some who were confident of their own righteousness and looked down on everybody else, Jesus told this parable" (Luke 18:9). What a perfect description of self-righteous people. They not only were "confident of their own righteousness"; these people also "looked down on everybody else." When one operates on his own standards, which are purely arbitrary, he is so self-centered and self-righteous that he becomes dissatisfied with everyone around him. No one comes up to his expectations or achieves his degree of excellence. Everyone who does not agree with him is wrong—and he ends up despising everyone but a chosen few in his "inner circle."

As we move along in the parable, Jesus gives us some other interesting insights into this kind of person. Let's look at a few of these idiosyncrasies: "Two men went up to the temple to pray, one a Pharisee and the other a tax collector. The Pharisee stood up and prayed about himself: 'God, I thank you that I am not like other men—robbers, evildoers, adulterers—or even like this tax collector' " (Luke 18:10-11). That's an interesting sidelight. "He prayed about himself." Prayer is supposed to start out with praise—praise of God. But this man was praising himself for what he himself was. Since he had done nothing wrong, he had nothing for which to repent. Instead he gloried in himself: "I fast twice a week and give a tenth of all I get" (v. 12). He goes on to pat himself on the back for keeping every one of the religious observances. Since he is completely self-righteous, he has no one to praise but himself. He is a classic example of what Jesus is talking about in Matthew 6. What an empty shell he is.

Now let's look at his companion, the tax collector. Suddenly we realize that he is everything Jesus was commending in these early verses of Matthew 6, where he calls for true piety to be reflected in quiet, unostentatious worship. In Luke 18:13 Jesus describes this man for us in depth: "But the tax collector stood at a distance. He would not even look up to heaven, but beat his breast and said, 'God, have mercy on me, a sinner.' " What a contrast! The first man prayed about himself, but this penitent person addressed himself to God, without daring to lift up so much as his eyes, let alone parade his life before the Father. What was God's reaction to these two men? Jesus spelled it out in verse 14: "I tell you that this man, rather than the other, went home justified before God. For everyone who exalts himself will be humbled, and he who humbles himself will be exalted."

This parable illustrates the peril of ostentatious "public" religion. We fall into the error of thinking that if we give to charity, the giving becomes and end in itself. We become spiritual exhibitionists; instead of giving from a humble, contrite heart, we give proudly and harshly, judgmentally perhaps. When that happens, the righteous of God is not operative in our lives.

The phrase "to be seen by them" in Matthew 6:1 comes from an interesting word in the Greek, a word from which we get our word *theater.* Those who give out of wrong motives are like actors on a stage. They are nothing more than exhibitionists. Not only are they guilty of theatrical charity, they are also guilty of "trumpet" charity: "So when you give to the needy, do not announce it with trumpets, as the hypocrites do in the synagogues and on the streets, to be honored by men" (Matt. 6:2). For them there awaits also the awful peril of elimination. When they stand before the judgment seat of God, and he asks them, "What did you do?" they will answer, "I gave ten million dollars to charity." But God will ask again, "What did you do?" They will reply, "I gave ten million dollars . . ." But God will interrupt, "No, you don't understand. I'm asking what you did of eternal significance. You didn't give out of a broken, contrite heart as the tax collector did. You didn't do it because it was a product of my righteousness in you. You gave it out of a self-righteous spirit. You have had your reward in the applause of men." That's the awful peril of exhibitionism.

The Promise of Reward

Do you know what the Bible says on this score? First of all, there is an initial reward. In Acts 20:35 Paul quotes the Lord Jesus when he says, "In everything I did, I showed you that by this kind of hard work we must help the weak, remembering the words the Lord Jesus himself said: 'It is more blessed to give than to receive.'" Do you know why many people do not have much blessing in their lives? Because the principle of blessing is in giving rather than receiving. There is an initial reward for anyone who becomes involved in charity, in giving, as a product of righteousness. The blessing that comes from such an outlook on life is immeasurable.

There is also an eternal reward for a giving spirit. Paul indicates this in 1 Corinthians 3:13-14: "His work will be shown for what it is, because the Day will bring it to light. It will be revealed with fire, and the fire will test the quality of each man's work. If what he has built survives, he will receive his reward." This scene will take place at the judgment seat of Christ. As you and I stand there, God will check on what we have done individually in the body. Wood, hay, and stubble will go up in smoke. Gold, silver, and precious stones will be refined in the fire, and based on these we will receive our reward.

Each one of us must ask ourselves on what we are basing our righteousness. Is it self-righteousness? Or unrighteousness? Each one of us must repent and receive God's righteousness in Christ. Are we letting our good works "shine" and glorify our Father in heaven? Have we had a conversion experience which is on display? Is there a communion of saints which is on display? Have we confessed with our mouth that Jesus is the Christ to the glory of God? Have we shown charity to those in need around us—whether their need be physical, spiritual, or emotional? As I fulfill Christ's admonition to true charity, I bring glory to him.

MAKING IT PRACTICAL

1. What happens when we try to "get" righteousness by doing righteous things?

2. How can our giving be truly righteous rather than merely self-righteous?

3. What are some appropriate ways for our righteousness to be displayed? How can we keep it from being hypocritical?

4. What do you learn, from the contrast between the Pharisee and the publican, about what pleases God?

5. What are some practical ways we can keep our motives and our actions pure when we give to the needy?

Therefore I tell you, Do not worry about your life, what you will eat or drink; or about your body, what you will wear. Is not life more important than food, and the body more important than clothes? Look at the birds of the air; they do not sow or reap or store away in barns, and yet your heavenly Father feeds them. Are you not much more valuable than they? Who of you by worrying can add a single hour to his life?

And why do you worry about clothes? See how the lilies of the field grow. They do not labor or spin. Yet I tell you that not even Solomon in all his splendor was dressed like one of these. If that is how God clothes the grass of the field, which is here today and tomorrow is thrown into the fire, will he not much more clothe you, O you of little faith? So do not worry, saying "What shall we eat?" or "What shall we drink?" or "What shall we wear?" For the pagans run after all these things, and your heavenly Father knows that you need them. But seek first his kingdom and his righteousness, and all these things will be given to you as well. Therefore do not worry about tomorrow. For tomorrow will worry about itself. Each day has enough trouble of its own.

Matthew 6:25-34

15
Anxiety

We began this book with an in-depth look at the Beatitudes. You may remember that all these verses began with the word *blessed*—which is another word for happy or joyful. We called it *Makarios* living. In a sense, Jesus is reminding his hearers of the truths with which he began his sermon as he moves into the subject of anxiety.

Let's look back for a moment. As we have been examining the Sermon on the Mount, we have been discovering how the Lord Jesus sets out all the motivational factors that are so important in our behavior patterns. Each one of us has a philosophy for life, and we all have distinctive lifestyles as a result of these motivations. Jesus intended that his followers should have a distinctive lifestyle because it was based on a distinctive philosophy of life, different from that of pagans, those not committed to living for the Lord.

As a result of this commitment to Christ, we would expect the Christian to live a different type of life, to perform differently. As Jesus said, we are to be the salt of the earth, the light of the world. We are to stand out in the world, not to be swept up by it.

What is one of the outstanding characteristics of our world today? I believe it is an overriding anxiety. That was the spirit Jesus was addressing in this passage. Notice how he repeats the idea of worrying about the future. Literally, he was urging his hearers not to be anxious concerning material things. In The Living Bible, these verses say:

> Don't worry about *things*—food, drink, money [implied], and clothes. For you already have life and a body—and they are far more important than what to eat and wear. Look at the birds! They don't worry about what to eat—they don't need to sow or reap or store up food—for your heavenly Father feeds them. And you are far more valuable to him than they are. Will all your worries add a single moment to your life? And why worry about your clothes? Look at the field lilies! They don't worry about theirs. . . . So don't worry at all about having enough food and clothing. *Matthew 6:25-31*

We need a clear definition of anxiety and worry. There is a fine line between being careless and not being careful. It seems that some people have taken Jesus' admonition to mean that carelessness and irresponsibility are to be the hallmarks of faith. I do not believe that is what he meant when he said not to worry. But he is saying that we are not to be engulfed by a foreboding sense of anxiety as we face each day. Have you ever seen an anxious person who also exuded a spirit of joy? Yet both Paul and Jesus admonished the early Christians to be joyful. I don't read that either teacher taught that Christians are to show a fearful or anxious spirit. One of the shades of meaning in the word *blessed,* which prefaces each of the Beatitudes, is the idea of being joyful.

Over and over again the New Testament tells us that the hallmark of the Christian life is to be a joyous spirit. How can we be joyful if our souls are riddled with anxiety and worry? This is the idea Jesus was seeking to convey here. Along with freeing us from the penalty of our sin at Calvary, Jesus also gave us the key to the marvelous freedom of a joyful spirit. This joy or happiness does not come to us because we make it the object of our pursuit. Rather, it is the by-product of the Christian life. As C. S. Lewis so aptly put it, we are "surprised by joy" when we yield control of our lives to the Master. Joy doesn't come from desperate seeking—it comes as a result of self-surrender.

Positive Concerns

As I've already pointed out, Paul also addressed this subject:

> I would like you to be free from concern. An unmarried man is concerned about the Lord's affairs—how he can please the Lord. But a married man is concerned about the affairs of this world—how he can please his wife—and his interests are divided. An unmarried woman or virgin is concerned about the Lord's affairs: Her aim is to be devoted to the Lord in both body and spirit. But a married woman is concerned about the affairs of this world—how she can please her husband.
>
> *1 Corinthians 7:32-34*

Notice how frequently Paul used the word *concern* in this passage. Notice, too, how he applauds those who are single. So often in our day, married people tend to feel sorry for those who are single—and some single people, too, feel sorry for themselves. But Paul sees this single state as a blessed condition, a special quality. Too often we neglect that concept. But that is not the main point of this passage. The essence of his thought here is that concern in certain areas is to be commended. Jesus was not urging his followers to be unconcerned about the work of the Lord. Neither does he condemn valid concern for marital responsibility. On the contrary, Paul's thought here is that if we are married, we are to accept our responsibilities and concerns. Concern in marriage is commended by Paul and by Jesus.

Later, in 1 Corinthians 12:25, Paul touches on this subject of concern once again: "There should be no division in the body, but . . . its parts should have equal concern for each other." Anxiety is condemned by the Lord, but real concern for others is commended by the Scriptures. This tension is necessary in the Christian pilgrimage. Too often, we Christians pride ourselves on the absence of anxiety from our lives—but we are not concerned for others either. It takes a certain degree of maturity to have the right kind of concern while struggling to overcome improper anxieties. 'If I lack concern for the physical and spiritual welfare of my fellow believers, I am simply being irresponsible.

Paul touched on this subject again in his second letter to the Corinthians: "Besides everything else, I face daily the pressure of my concern for all the churches" (2 Cor. 11:28). The same man who wrote, "Do not be anxious about anything" (Phil. 4:6) admits here that he is concerned for his churches. The Living Bible gives this thought as "I have the constant worry of how the churches are getting along." Paul condemns anxiety, as Jesus did, but he commends concern—in marriage, in membership, and in ministry. He brings it up again in Philippians 2:20: "I have no one else like him, who takes a genuine interest in your welfare." Paul was looking for someone who cared enough, who was concerned enough, to go on a mission for him to Philippi—and he could find no one.

Apply that lesson to our situation in the church of Jesus Christ today. What has happened to our concern for others, our mission to the unreached world around us? Yes, anxiety was to be condemned (both Paul and Jesus make this truth clear), but concern for others is to be commended.

Negative Concerns

Let's look back again at the Sermon on the Mount: "Therefore I tell you, do not worry about your life" (Matt. 6:25). Jesus has put his finger on our problem when he says, "for *your* life." Self-centered, egocentric concern for self is at the heart of our problem today. Concern for others is commendable, but anxiety for our own well-being is condemned. The Greek word for "life" as translated here is an interesting word. It's the word from which we get *psychic, psychology,* and *psychiatrist.* In other words, it has to do with our own personhood, our own being. Jesus is simply saying we should not be riddled by anxiety for our own well-being.

Another area of anxiety lies in the matter of family *finances*. Jesus touched on that just before launching into his discussion of anxiety: "Do not store up for yourselves treasures on earth, where moth and rust destroy, and where thieves break in and steal. But store up for yourselves treasures in heaven, where moth and rust do not destroy, and where thieves do not break in and steal. For where your treasure is, there your heart will be also" (Matt. 6:19-21). There's one simple solution to this problem of making ends meet—and that is to spend slightly less than you make. I must say to myself, "God has graciously blessed me with the ability to earn this much, so he must want me to live at this level. I will simply live within the confines of what I earn." That philosophy will solve the financial worries of some people.

Others have an opposite problem when it comes to worry about money. They have so much that they don't know what to do with it. They would say, "The Lord has given me so much that I am worried about holding on to it." For them, the love of money has become the root of all evil. The answer to this kind of problem is to realize that we are merely stewards of what we possess. We should take the attitude that none of this wealth is ours, but that is has been entrusted to us by our Father. We are merely to be conduits of his blessing to others. Our prayer should be, "Father, please give me wisdom to know how much I should keep for myself, and how to channel the rest for your glory."

So we have two kinds of anxiety about money: If we have it, we worry about keeping it; and if we don't have it, we worry about getting it. Financial concerns are certainly a problem for most of us.

Another area of anxiety Jesus touched upon was this matter of *food:* "Do not worry about your life, what you will eat or drink" (v. 25). As I look around in the United States, I don't see many of us worried about the amount of food we have. True, there are pockets of poverty in our country where people don't have enough food to eat, and many of these are children. But a more widespread problem lies in the problem of *over*eating. But as we look to other parts of the world, we see the awful fingers of famine stretching across the African continent, and we sense the concern Jesus was voicing here. For his hearers were facing a daily struggle for sufficient food, much as do the people in the third world today. Anxiety about food was a real temptation for them.

Jesus condemned undue concern for *fashion* along with undue concern for finances and food. Here is a prohibition that hits our fashion-conscious world. One of our largest industries is the clothing industry, which speaks of the concern most people have about being fashionably dressed.

This leads me to the area of *fitness*. All across our country health spas have sprung up almost overnight, catering to people's undue concern about physical fitness. Don't get me wrong—I'm not critical about normal care for our bodies, for they are a God-given gift. But I do think Americans have made a fad of physical fitness. Conversely, they don't seem particularly interested in using their bodies for the glory of God or in reaching out to others in need. Theirs is a self-seeking search for fitness so that they might worship at the shrine of human beauty. Their primary purpose in keeping fit is to help themselves rather than their fellow human beings.

The *future* is also a subject of undue concern for many people today. Jesus was dealing with that anxiety when he said, "Who of you by worrying can add a single hour to his life?" (Matt. 6:27). This concern lies at the heart of the current and continuing popularity of shallow and sensational prophetic preaching today. Again, don't get me wrong. I'm in favor of biblical preaching, the presentation of the whole counsel of God—but I have problem with some of the practitioners of the fine art of "snowing" gullible people with speculation and date-setting. Here again, this kind of preaching panders to the self-concern of people, which Jesus is condemning in no uncertain terms.

Anxiety will kill our joy in the Lord and restrict our liberty. Valid concern for others is one thing (commended by our Lord), but selfish anxiety is soundly criticized and condemned by him.

Christ's Attitude toward Anxiety

First of all, Jesus made it clear that anxiety is an exercise in futility: "Who of you by worrying can add a single hour to his life?" (Matt. 6:27). No matter how much we worry, no matter how concerned we are, we cannot do anything about what God has ordained. I believe that our times are in his hand—and nothing I can do will change that.

Secondly, anxiety shows our lack of faith in God: "If that is how God clothes the grass of the field, which is here today and tomorrow is thrown into the fire, will he not much more clothe you, O you of little faith?" (Matt. 6:30). I would hate for Jesus to call me "one of little faith." But that's who I am if I doubt for one minute his ability to take care of me, if I show anxiety in my self-centered concern for number one.

"Look," Jesus is saying, "I made your body, and I made your personhood. If I'm able to make them, I'm certainly capable of keeping them going. So don't get all concerned about survival and worried about yourself. If you believe I made you, then you have no alternative but to believe that I will work out my purposes for you." If I believe that after making me and sustaining me all these years God is going to suddenly withdraw his upholding power, I have a peculiar view of God. I am showing that I believe he can be unfaithful. This concept of God is what Jesus is flatly condemning here.

Jesus uses two illustrations of his care for us: "Look at the birds of the air" and "see how the lilies of the field grow" (Matt. 6:26, 28). I have often wondered if a bird may have flown out of some cover near the crowd when Jesus spoke these words—or if there were lilies growing in the field where they were standing. Maybe that's why he used the sudden word *look* in referring to the restless birds, and the quiet word *see* in calling to their attention this expression of his creative powers. God is both startling (as is the bird who suddenly flies from cover) and steady (as is the lily quietly blooming where it is planted) in his care.

The Christian Answer to Anxiety

First of all, the Christian answer to anxiety is to *accept God's providence.* The passage we have been considering in this chapter begins with the word "therefore," and when I see that word I ask myself, "What's it there for?" Three times Jesus repeats it, in verses 25, 31, and 34. (The NIV leaves it out of vs. 31.) The word "therefore" is a link between what has gone by and what is coming. It's not enough simply to tell people not to be anxious. Let's look at each instance.

In verse 25, the "therefore" refers to what was said in verse 24: "No one can serve two masters. Either he will hate the one and love the other, or he will be devoted to the one and despise the other. You cannot serve both God and Money." If I've decided to *serve God and not money,* then there is no need to be anxious. God accepts full responsibility for me if I've come to the place of saying, "God, my times are in your hands. I don't know what the future holds for me, but I know who holds my future." From this perspective I can be confident that as I serve the living and true God, I know his providence in my heart. If I rely on God's providence, I can be certain of his provision.

In verse 31, the "therefore" follows the reference to the birds of the air and the lilies of the field. If God is able to take care of small things, he can certainly handle the big matters, Jesus is saying. After all, man was God's crowning creation. He will not let him down.

In verse 34, Jesus is reflecting again upon motivation. If we *put the kingdom of God first,* we do not need to be overly concerned with the future. Base your life on God's priorities, Jesus says, and you will have no cause for anxiety. If you live this way, you can anticipate the divine promises summed up in verse 33: "Seek first his kingdom and his righteousness, and all these things will be given to you as well."

The fourth thing is to apply the divine principle. A paraphrase of verse 34 might be *"Live one day at a time."* This applies the principle Jesus was expressing. This is the Christian answer to anxiety. Succumbing to anxiety, on the other hand, will reduce the Christian to the lifestyle of the unbeliever. Overcome by anxiety, we fail to represent our Savior as we should. This is why Jesus tells us, "Do not worry. . . ."

MAKING IT PRACTICAL

1. What are some of the things that might cause us to believe that "an overriding anxiety" is one of the outstanding characteristics of our world today?

2. What is the relationship between joy and anxiety?

3. What do you think of the author's statement that "Too often, we Christians pride ourselves on the absence of anxiety from our lives—but we are not concerned for others either." What is the distinction between worry and a good kind of concern?

4. What are some other areas of life about which we worry, not listed in this passage? What do you think Jesus would say to these issues?

5. What has God done to remind you that you don't need to be anxious because he will take care of you?

6. What are some practical ways we can remind ourselves not to be unduly anxious? What are some reminders we might post in strategic places in our home, office, car, etc.? Where in particular would it be important for you to place reminders?

Do not store up for yourselves treasures on earth, where moth and rust destroy, and where thieves break in and steal. But store up for yourselves treasures in heaven, where moth and rust do not destroy, and where thieves do not break in and steal. For where your treasure is, there your heart will be also.

So do not worry, saying, "What shall we eat?" or "What shall we drink?" or "What shall we wear?" For the pagans run after all these things, and your heavenly Father knows that you need them. But seek first his kingdom and his righteousness, and all these things will be given to you as well.

Matthew 6:19-21; 31-33

16
Priorities

Let's remember that in the Sermon on the Mount Jesus is calling for his followers to live according to a distinctive lifestyle, guided by a distinctive philosophy rooted in the eternal Word of God. One of the tensions we encounter as Christians is the constant bombardment of conflicting philosophies in total opposition to the truth as we know it in the Bible. And one of our biggest problems in this topsy-turvy world is to recognize our priorities.

Discovering Our Priorities

We have all been encouraged to "put first things first." The problem is to discover what is first. All kinds of demands are placed on the Christian. Deep in our hearts we know we need to put first things first, but with all the voices, all the different ideas and philosophies vying for our attention, we struggle to determine what should really be first. It's relatively easy to say, "Major on the major, and minor on the minor"—but the difficulty lies in determining what is minor. It's really a matter of constant reevaluation.

Let me get personal for a moment. I have a real problem establishing priorities. As a pastor, believe it or not, I have had people concerned for my physical welfare. They have encouraged me to make physical fitness a priority. Some of the people were also concerned about my prayer life. They had been reading about Martin Luther, who made it a practice to spend several hours at prayer in the early hours of the day—and they wondered how I fared in that regard! Someone else in the congregation felt that I might be neglecting my own family because of my devotion to the people in the church. Another person (who was concerned that I be in touch with what is going on in the world around me) gave me a membership in a book club!

There are other pressures on me as a pastor. Some people think I am away from my pulpit too much—away from my family. On the other hand, I have a stack of mail inviting me to speak here and speak there—wonderful opportunities to minister the Word. What do I do? How do I arrive at the proper priorities? How do I keep from neglecting my work at home as I respond to these opportunities that come my way for ministering away from home? the answer is simple but difficult to carry out. I must recognize my priorities.

Some people are well-organized in this regard. They make a list, one—two—three. But you may not be that kind of person. I can make a list all right—but then I lose the list! So our answer must lie outside ourselves—in the Word of God. When Jesus talks about our priorities, he's interested in three areas of our lives: our activities, our anxieties, and our ambitions. Let's go back to the Sermon on the Mount to discover his guidelines in this area. In Matthew 6:19 Jesus said, "Do not store up for yourselves treasures on earth." Jesus is speaking to all of us in these incisive words.

There is no better way to measure our priorities than to look at our *activities*. Our activities translate into priorities—and Jesus has some very pungent things to say about our activities and the way they determine our priorities. We have already dealt with some of these matters in the earlier chapters of this book.

Our *anxieties* are also a gauge of our priorities. In verse 25 Jesus said, "Therefore I tell you, do not worry about your life, what you will eat or drink; or about your body, what you will wear." We all have anxieties, and Jesus touched on most of them here, dealing with finances, food, fashion, fitness, and the future. The things I am anxious about are the things that take priority in my life. If we are going to get our priorities right, it is very important that we begin to recognize what our existing priorities are. If we are having trouble in our spiritual lives, it's probably because we have our priorities all mixed up. By checking on our activities and our anxieties we will soon discover what these priorities are.

The word *seek* in Matthew 6 gives us a clue to our *ambitions,* which are another indication of our priorities: "For the pagans *run after* all these things, and your heavenly Father knows that you need them. But *seek* first his kingdom and his righteousness, and all these things will be given to you as well" (vv. 32-33, italics mine). The word *seek* conveys the idea of desire, the concept of intense ambition and endeavor. When Jesus talks about what people are seeking for or running after, he is basically talking about their ambitions. Ambition is a strange and fascinating attribute. Too much ambition can ruin a person—but lack of ambition can be just as disastrous.

Ambition can be very destructive if it is simply egocentric. One of the problems in the business world today lies in this very area. People who "want what they want" so intensely that they will do anything to reach their goal can ruin lives around them. Getting to the top of the pile is more important to them than the people they must step on to get there. And these same people will also destroy themselves in the process of reaching the top. They drive themselves beyond endurance in their ambition to get to the pinnacle of success.

On the opposite end of the scale is the person who makes a virtue of scorning ambition. Someone without ambition of any kind is less than human. He is an insult to the God who made him because he has no intensity of desire to be what he was made to be.

It boils down to priorities again. If I am totally ambitious to the point of being self-centered, I can blow my life apart with the destructive forces at work in me. Or if I lack ambition, I can throw my life away.

Our next step is to determine which of our priorities are most important.

Rating Our Priorities

Jesus addressed priorities in Matthew 6:19-20 when he said, "Do not store up for yourselves treasures on earth, where moth and rust destroy, and where thieves break in and steal. But store up for yourselves treasures in heaven, where moth and rust do not destroy, and where thieves do not break in and steal." What was Jesus saying?

Rating our activities

Measure your activities in the light of eternity. Use your God-given raw materials (your strength, skills, time, and energy) according to priorities set forth by God himself. It is terribly easy to devote ourselves to activities not remotely related to eternity. We can live our earthly lives without "storing up" any heavenly treasure. And when we leave the earthly treasure we have amassed, what happens? It remains for the moths and rust to feed upon. And when we reach our heavenly destination, we have nothing there—we are utterly and totally destitute, having swallowed the false success story syndrome and devoted ourselves to earthly pursuits.

It may sound as if I am saying that so-called secular activity, working in a bank, if you will, is wrong for a Christian. After all, I left the banking business for the ministry. No, that's not what I am saying at all. What we must do, regardless of our type of activity, is to perform our tasks in light of eternity. It is possible to be deeply involved in all kinds of activities without giving a thought to God at all. If that is the case, our activities are showing that our priorities are basically mundane. We must rate our activities in the light of eternity.

Rating our anxieties

Another way to rate our priorities is to check on our anxieties. In verse 32 Jesus urges us to look at our needs from God's perspective, realizing that he can and will supply all our needs according to his riches in glory. Our lifestyles and our priorities are determined by our attitude toward God's ability to supply our needs. I must live my life in the light of one tremendous fact: My heavenly Father knows my needs and is abundantly able to meet them. If I am anxious about many things, as Martha was, I will miss my Father's best for me. Rating my anxieties will show me clearly whether or not I believe in the providence of God—his ability to care for me.

Rating our ambitions

Seek first the kingdom of God, Jesus tells us in verse 33. What a superb statement. This puts our activities and anxieties into perspective, doesn't it? Most of us would have to admit that we hardly know what the kingdom of God is, let alone knowing how to put it first!

There are two things about the kingdom of God which we should notice. First of all, it must be *experienced*. In John 3 we meet a man called Nicodemus, a ruler of the Jews, highly articulate, well educated—a leader among men, highly respected. He was at the top of the political and academic world of his day. Nicodemus had heard of this young carpenter who came from Nazareth, and he was interested in what Jesus had to say. He even called Jesus "Rabbi" (John 3:2), a title of respect that mirrored his attitude toward this man from Nazareth.

Jesus doesn't bother with small talk as this respected leader of the Jews comes to him. He gets right to the root of the ruler's problem: "I tell you the truth, no one can see the kingdom of God unless he is born again" (John 3:3). There's that term again—the kingdom of God. And what Jesus said here may be applied not only to Nicodemus, but to everyone. In order to experience the kingdom of God, we must be born again. On the authority of the Word of God, if I have not been born again, I cannot be a member of the kingdom of God. This must be *first* if our priorities are going to be in line with God's plan.

This concept applies to our ambitions as well. If my goal in life is to be "born again," then I will not get hung up on lesser things like becoming an All-American—or a millionaire. If becoming a member of his kingdom is my first priority, then all the other aspects of my life will fall into proper perspective.

This leads to another thought. Once the kingdom of God has been experienced, it must also be *expressed*. This was what Paul was writing about in 1 Corinthians 4:19-20: "But I will come to you very soon, if the Lord is willing, and then I will find out not only how these people are talking, but what power they have. For the kingdom of God is not a matter of talk but of power." What was he saying? Simply this: the kingdom of God is not talk, it's dynamite! The kingdom of God is expressed in powerful living. The kingdom of God is right here and now! It's not some nebulous something out there in the future somewhere. Therefore my priority must be to demonstrate the power of God here and now. I must not be swept up in the secular thinking around me. I must not be swallowed up by the false ambitions of my contemporaries who surround me. Rather, I must be totally involved in the *kingdom*. That is the message Jesus is seeking to convey here. If my priority is to survive in the business world, or to make it socially, then I may miss the kingdom. The kingdom must be experienced and expressed. "And this gospel of the kingdom will be preached in the whole world as a testimony to all nations, and then the end will come" (Matt. 24:14). Any Christian who understands the commitment of Jesus Christ to see the eternal kingdom established in the lives of people from every tribe and tongue and nation will have no difficulty recognizing that he or she has a part to play in this extension ministry. And it will become a priority!

Relating Our Priorities

We have recognized our priorities and rated them—now we must relate them. How do we do this? Jesus told us that our concern should not be for earthly treasure, but for heavenly. Are my financial priorities earthly or heavenly? How do I handle my paycheck? Have I written across it, "First the kingdom"? My checks have pictures on them—perhaps yours do, too. Wouldn't it be great if our checks could have a picture of heaven on them, to remind us to put the kingdom first? Or what if they could have pictures of hungry people on them? Wouldn't that remind us of proper priorities in terms of our finances?

First the kingdom. That means I am going to apply eternal concepts to earthly affairs and activities. If I'm going to be a Christian and invest my time, strength, and energy for eternity, I may have to look upon certain activities not in terms of what is wrong with them—but in terms of "What is the point?" I can't excuse my activities by saying they are not harming anyone. Instead, I must ask myself what good am I doing? What am I accomplishing? This is applying the concept of the eternal to the earthly.

I must also apply the concept of providence to my problems. Is my overriding concern to protect all that I have, or am I prepared to trust God and take some steps of faith?

Then I must apply the concept of the spiritual to the secular. Even the most mundane activity must be done "as unto the Lord." Are my priorities in line with my eternal orientation? In my activities, anxieties, and ambitions, do I have an overriding concern that the kingdom of God be experienced by all kinds of people? Above all other concerns, do I desire that his kingdom be extended? Is that the way my priorities are arranged? If that's the case, I will have obeyed Jesus' admonition to seek first the kingdom of God.

MAKING IT PRACTICAL

1. Practically speaking, what does it mean to "seek first God's kingdom"?

2. How do our activities, our anxieties, and our ambitions show what our priorities truly are?

3. As you look around you, what do people in our society seem to "run after," worry about, and spend most of their time doing? How about the church? What does that tell you about their priorities?

4. What is your number-one priority? How is that reflected in your ambitions, anxieties, and actions?

5. What are some specific ways we can "store up treasure" in heaven? What did Jesus mean when he said that in heaven, "moth and rust do not destroy, and thieves do not break in and steal"?

6. How does your life presently reflect eternal priorities? In what ways would you like it to even more?

Enter through the narrow gate. For wide is the gate and broad is the road that leads to destruction, and many enter through it. But small is the gate and narrow the road that leads to life, and only a few find it.

Matthew 7:13-14

17
Discipline

It is not uncommon for the world to accuse Christians of being narrow. This is not an accusation. In a sense, it is a compliment. If narrow means that I have a magnificent obsession, a total and inflexible commitment to a person—Jesus Christ—then I plead guilty! I will not deviate from the way in which I am walking with him, no matter how narrow that way.

Actually, narrowness can be a virtue. Take the ground lights that tell the pilot where the airfield is. They can be approached from 360° all the way around the horizon—but only one angle of approach is right. It is the pilot's business to bring his giant aircraft in on that exact angle. It reminds me of the words of the Lord: "This is the way; walk in it" (Isa. 30:21). It takes special discipline to produce this attention to detail, this narrowness of vision that assures us we are on the path that God would choose for us.

The Discipline of Discernment

Some people are perfectly happy to justify their lifestyle by saying, "Everybody's doing it." Such people are guilty of lazy thinking—complete lack of the discipline of discernment. Another approach to life is to say, "If you like it, it must be right." Others blandly affirm, "We're all headed in the same direction, and it really doesn't matter what we believe just as long as we are sincere." This sounds loving and beautiful—but it is a prime example of the kind of fuzzy-headed thinking permeating our world today. It is completely contrary to the lifestyle advocated by the Lord Jesus, which called for discipline.

If we live in a society producing people who never bother to think through to what they really believe and why they believe it, then we are a part of a society that is headed for oblivion. Jesus presented us with alternatives that in turn call for discernment as we make our choices in life. Look at some of these alternatives.

First of all, Jesus talked about the two ends of existence: eternal life and eternal destruction. If our thinking patterns are fuzzy and indefinite, we will not be concerned about issues such as these. Such decisions take discernment—and that quality is completely lacking in the life that takes a don't-care attitude. Simply drifting with the current or blowing with the wind is easy—but it is the path that leads to destruction. If we are going to stand for the truth as it is in Jesus, we must buck the stream, we must be willing to struggle against the lethargy around us.

Jesus also talked about two ways to go: the broad and the narrow. It's easier to drift downstream with the crowd than it is to enter at the small gate. What did Jesus mean when he talked about the narrow road "that leads to life"? He clarified that statement in John 10:10 when he said: "I have come that they may have life, and have it to the full." This life he came to give was his own life—resurrection life! Paul said, "For the wages of sin is death, but the gift of God is eternal life in Christ Jesus our Lord" (Romans 6:23). The Bible is full of this message; it is thrillingly possible to experience eternal life here and now.

Eternal life is not something you get when you die if you have been good enough. Eternal life is maturity now—being and doing what God calls us to be and do *now!* Once you have taken that step of faith, you have been invaded by the resurrection life of Jesus himself. Jesus Christ is alive and well in the lives of committed

Christians! I am enriched by his indwelling presence *now!* Near the close of his Gospel John wrote, "But these are written that you may believe that Jesus is the Christ, the Son of God, and that by believing you may *have* life in his name" (John 20:31, italics mine). How much clearer could it be?

What is the alternative to eternal life? The Bible has many words for it, but one is *perishing:* "If our gospel is veiled, it is veiled to those who are perishing" (2 Cor. 4:3). The alternative to eternal life is living a wasted life, being totally lost, perishing. The opposite of eternal life is a life headed for destruction. This is the only alternative to eternal life. In 1 John 5:13 the evangelist says, "I write these things to you who believe in the name of the Son of God so that you may know that you have eternal life." Eternal life and eternal destruction are opposite ends of human society. The person who will perish is already perishing. The one who will one day stand before God with a wasted life is at this very moment busy wasting it. Just as truly, the one who has eternal life awaiting him is already living that life!

The key to the whole matter lies in commitment. If we commit ourselves to God's way, the narrow path, if you will, eternal life is already ours. If we commit ourselves to the "broad . . . road that leads to destruction," our destiny is determined. The choice is ours. The promise of eternal life awaits those who follow Jesus' admonition to "Follow me." Where is he going? Jesus said, "As long as it is day, we must do the work of him who sent me. Night is coming, when no one can work" (John 9:4). This is the narrow way. He also said, "In a little while you will see me no more, and then after a little while you will see me" (John 16:16). There is no question about where he is going.

The problem in the church today is not lack of direction. The problem is that people fail to follow Jesus. People want to avoid destruction certainly—but they are not ready to commit themselves unreservedly to the Savior. That's why the church is ineffective. A Christian is to be disciplined, a disciple who follows the narrow way. Instead, the church is filled with people who want to take the "broad" way, who want to follow the philosophy expressed in

Judges 21:25—"In those days Israel had no king; everyone did as he saw fit." The Bible makes it clear that this was the stage when the nation of Israel began to come apart at the seams.

Paul describes the same scene in more recent times: "having a form of godliness but denying its power" (2 Tim. 3:5). This is what I call the "broad way" approach to life—individualism gone mad, people refusing and rejecting God's disciplined way of life, insisting on doing their own thing and going their own way.

Christians simply must be able to discriminate and discern God's way—and then have the discipline to follow it. Jesus said, "I am the way and the truth and the life. No one comes to the Father except through me" (John 14:6). This is the small gate of discipleship. It reminds me of my experience in Bethlehem, entering the Church of the Nativity. As is often my practice, I was so busy talking I wasn't looking where I was going. As we entered the church I failed to notice the height of the entrance. It's a small gate about four feet high. I left quite an impression in that hard rock with my head! That small gate is the main entrance to that great barn of a church. What a graphic illustration of the "small gate" Jesus was talking about here in Matthew 7!

Universalism is basically the doctrine that a God of love would never allow anyone to go to destruction, and therefore everyone is ultimately going to be saved. This "wide gate" assumption has crept into the church today, crippling its effectiveness, watering down its message.

Despite the smallness of the gate that leads to life, to heaven itself, there will be multitudes of true disciples there. It is easy to get the impression that Christians are few and far between here in this world. Ask any student or businessman about his experiences—does he stand alone? Many times it seems that he does. We are all tempted to feel that we are the only follower of Jesus Christ in our particular sphere of influence. But rather than think of ourselves as the *only* follower, we should think of ourselves as the *first* follower—in our families, in our offices, wherever we are.

The Discipline of Decision

This discipline relates not only to the *gate* at which we enter (our initial commitment to Jesus Christ), but it also relates to the *road* we follow, the ongoing experience of Jesus Christ. There is a difference. Think of it this way. It doesn't take long to *get married*—but it takes many years to *be married*. It doesn't take long to sign a mortgage agreement to buy a house—but it may take twenty-five years or more to pay off that mortgage. In the same way, it doesn't take long to make the initial commitment to Jesus Christ, repenting of sin, deciding to follow the Savior. But that is just the beginning. Walking the narrow way after entering in at the small gate is daily saying yes to God and no to Satan.

"This is the way; walk in it," said Jesus. This takes the daily discipline of discipleship—daily obedience to God's commands. In Luke 13:24 Jesus gives us a slight variation on the "small gate" admonition: *"Make every effort* to enter through the narrow door, because many, I tell you, will try to enter and will not be able to" (italics mine). Have you ever seen anyone "sweat" his way into the kingdom? I have. It is somewhat perturbing to see the "easy believism" so prevalent in Christian circles today. It seems that some people simply "float" into the kingdom on notes of sweet music, easy emotionalism, and soft sentimentalism. Discipline doesn't enter into the picture at all. Many have made "valley" commitments—but have gone back to the old ways when their circumstances were altered. We used to call them "foxhole conversions."

Such commitments lack the discipline we have been suggesting in this chapter. The crucial problems arise after the initial commitment—and if that commitment has been made too lightly, too easily, then the follower begins to falter on the way, and in the daily battle begins to lose his way. This is what Jesus was warning against when he urged his followers to "strive" to enter in. Making a valid commitment to Jesus Christ involves daily decisions that may cause "spiritual perspiration." All this is involved in the discipline of decision: Quit fooling around, and give the Lord top priority in your life.

The Discipline of Discipleship

The word translated "narrow" here in Matthew 7:14 means something totally different from the word translated "small": "But small is the gate and narrow the road that leads to life, and only a few find it." The word translated "narrow" is variously translated elsewhere in the New Testament: "For he had healed many, so that those with diseases were *pushing forward* to touch him" (Mark 3:10, italics mine); this creates a picture in my mind of reporters pressing around trying to pick up a story. Celebrities and politicians are subjected to this kind of pressure—but so are Christians, so be ready. Another translation for "narrow" is "persecuted": "When we were with you, we kept telling you that we would be *persecuted*" (1 Thess. 3:4). Still another word for "narrow" is "troubles": "For our light and momentary troubles are achieving for us an eternal glory that far outweighs them all" (2 Cor. 4:17).

It takes discipline to be a disciple. The way of the disciple is a pressed-in way, a way of persecution and troubles. Jesus made that clear in Matthew 16:24-25: "If anyone would come after me, he must deny himself and take up his cross and follow me. For whoever wants to save his life will lose it, but whoever loses his life for me will find it." Discipleship costs! It means the narrow way of crucifixion or commitment. The disciple must deny himself and take up his cross. But it also means continuance, for the disciple is committed to follow Jesus—and he isn't standing still!

At first glance, this matter of discipleship sounds and appears frightening in its ramifications and scope. But there are promises for us pilgrims in the way. One in particular blesses my soul every time I contemplate it: "Come to me, all you who are weary and burdened, and I will give you rest. Take my yoke upon you and learn from me, for I am gentle and humble in heart, and you will find rest for your souls. For my yoke is easy and my burden is light" (Matt. 11:28-30). Jesus does not deny that discipleship is costly. There is a yoke, and there is a burden. But the beautiful thing about it is this: The yoke is "easy," and the burden is "light," because we take it up as a labor of love. It is amazing what we can do when we love someone. Mothers have been known to rush into burning houses to rescue their children—burning themselves cruelly in the process, but not even feeling the burns. Loving Jesus Christ supremely because he first loved me takes the drudgery out of discipleship, the pain out of commitment, and the fear out of following. That's why discipleship, while costly, is an "easy" yoke and a "light" burden.

MAKING IT PRACTICAL

1. In what ways is "narrow-mindedness" sometimes proper for the Christian?

2. What in our society contributes to fuzzy, indefinite thinking? How can we, as Christians, keep from "drifting with the tide" of undisciplined thought?

3. What are some specific ways we can take a stand for the truth?

4. What do you think of the author's statement that the problem in the church today is not lack of direction, but failure to follow? If you agree, what are some ways we might address this problem?

5. How are discipline and discipleship daily, moment-by-moment decisions?

6. How can his "yoke" be "easy" and his "burden" be "light"?

Watch out for false prophets. They come to you in sheep's clothing, but inwardly they are ferocious wolves. By their fruit you will recognize them. Do people pick grapes from thornbushes, or figs from thistles? Likewise every good tree bears good fruit, but a bad tree bears bad fruit. A good tree cannot bear bad fruit, and a bad tree cannot bear good fruit. Every tree that does not bear good fruit is cut down and thrown into the fire. Thus, by their fruit you will recognize them.

Matthew 7:15-20

18
Vigilance

Christians are called upon to be alert, to be aware of the enemies who lurk around us, ready to pounce upon us from our blind side. The alert Christian first of all realizes that he is *vulnerable*. Then, because he is aware of his vulnerability, he maintains *vigilance* in every area of his life. Finally, because of vulnerability and vigilance, he can be *victorious*.

Our Vulnerability

The Bible warns the believer about three main opponents: the world, the flesh, and the devil. Because these three powers come against us with such tremendous force, they represent the areas in which we are most vulnerable.

Satan

The Bible is quite clear in presenting this being as an absolute tyrant. People are taken "captive to do his will" (2 Tim. 2:26). Paul is specific in warning Timothy (and Christians today as well) that the devil is actively engaged in wrecking human lives. There is a personality of evil—Satan—just as definitely as there is a personality of good—God. One reason I believe this so strongly is that Satan confronted Jesus himself. This to me is the best evidence for the validity of the personhood of Satan.

Aware of Satan's activity, Paul warns us of the archdeceiver's devices: " . . . that Satan might not outwit us. For we are not unaware of his schemes" (2 Cor. 2:11). One reason for the church's current lack of effectiveness in the world lies in this very area—ignorance of Satan's devices. In fact, some would tell us that Satan is a medieval myth, a figment of our imagination. So why develop a strategy for defeating him?

This reminds me of my first experience with the American game of baseball. At first I didn't really understand what was happening on the field when the players shifted their position depending upon who was at bat. But then I learned that every batter has his strengths and weaknesses—and the fielders as well as the baseman and the pitcher compensated for these strengths or weaknesses by the way they played their position. This is the way to cope with Satan. Anticipate his moves before he makes them—and the battle is half won already. Be aware of his techniques. He, too, seeks to take advantage of our weaknesses—so if we are to successfully handle his attacks, we must know how he operates. How happy he is when we don't believe in his existence at all—for then he can have a field day with us!

In the light of this verse, how can we doubt his existence: "Be self-controlled and alert. Your enemy the devil prowls around like a roaring lion looking for someone to devour" (1 Pet. 5:8)? Beware, however. He doesn't always go around like a roaring lion. Sometimes he masquerades as an angel of light (2 Cor. 11:14). Sometimes Satan comes in the back door of subtlety rather than the front door of direct attack. If he cannot get us one way, he will try to reach us by another path.

Satan is also a liar: "When he lies, he speaks his native language, for he is a liar and the father of lies," Jesus warned in John 8:44. This is the person we are dealing with. Be alert and aware!

The world

A second traditional enemy of the believer is "the world." The problem down through the centuries has been to identify what is meant by the "world" in this context. At one point many felt that the word and the concept applied to "worldly amusements," dress standards in contemporary society, attitudes toward certain foods and drinks. According to the Scriptures, however, the "world" refers to the world system, the mindset, the philosophy prevalent in contemporary society. This broadens its meaning considerably.

In Ephesians 2:2 Paul refers to this concept: "You followed the ways of this world and of the ruler of the kingdom of the air, the spirit who is now at work in those who are disobedient." Here Paul is referring to an attitude, an approach toward life. It is so easy to be swept up into the thinking of the society in which we live. This insidious temptation to "go along" reminds me of a dead fish floating lazily downstream. Who wants to stand against the tide? Who wants to stand out as the oddball who goes contrary to the crowd? This is the subtle temptation against which the Christian must battle in his own particular segment of the world.

There is always a danger that the Christian may assume that his national lifestyle is "right," and he may even regard his cultural norms as more binding than biblical principles. In this way patriotism and nationalism can be quite contrary to Scripture and in actuality nothing more than worldliness. The only way to evaluate any system is to look at it in the light of the Word of God. It is all too easy to adopt a lifestyle that is contrary to what the Scriptures teach.

The sinful nature

The third enemy of whom we should be aware is our own sinful nature, the selfish attitude that resides within people, the flesh, the old nature, the power of sin, the part of us that is antagonistic to God and his demands upon us. Satan oversees the whole attack— with our sinful nature our enemy from within and the world system our enemy from without. If we are not alert to the presence of this enemy inside us, we will never understand how vulnerable we are in the spiritual realm. In 1790 the Lord Mayor of Dublin said, "The condition on which God hath given liberty to man is eternal vigilance."

In Galatians 5:17 Paul tells us, "For the sinful nature desires what is contrary to the Spirit, and the Spirit what is contrary to the sinful nature. They are in conflict with each other." This *world* is a battleground—and we Christians are at the heart of that battle! Anyone who thinks the Christian life is a bed of roses hasn't looked realistically at the battle lines drawn up all around us. In addition, the *Christian* is a battleground—and the warring factions are the sinful nature, which is antagonistic to the Spirit, and the Spirit of God, which is antagonistic to the sinful nature. Therefore, as Paul says, "The weapons we fight with are not the weapons of the world. On the contrary, they have divine power to demolish strongholds" (2 Cor. 10:4). On a more personal level he confessed, "We know that the law is spiritual; but I am unspiritual, sold as a slave to sin. I do not understand what I do, for what I want to do I do not do, but what I hate I do" (Rom. 7:14-15). Within me, says Paul, there is a constant battle raging.

Every Christian struggles through this battle. Many are concerned because of an occasional lapse back into the old life—and they should be. But they should not be discouraged, because their very concern about some wrong or questionable action is an indication of a new attitude, a new concern within them to do what is right. This is evidence of the new life within. One of the best indications that you have been born again by the Spirit of God is a growing discomfort about things that did not make you uncomfortable before.

Our Vigilance

Here in the Sermon on the Mount Jesus is not talking particularly about Satan. At the very outset he spells it out for us: "Watch out for false prophets" (Matt. 7:15). A prophet does two things: he foretells (predicts) and he forthtells (proclaims). Prophets are of two kinds: they represent God, or they are in total opposition to God. The Bible has much to say about false or pseudoprophets, and other false people (even the antichrist is a "false Christ"). We might also describe them as counterfeit. Jesus makes it clear that false prophets are of their father, the devil. They speak by this false spirit—this spirit of the antichrist—that comes straight from Satan himself. Such a prophet may give every indication of authority, of sincerity—but he reflects the spirit of his father the devil. As Jesus describes him, he comes "in sheep's clothing," but inwardly he is like a ferocious wolf.

How do we tell the false prophet from the true? Check out what he is saying—and look at the fruit of his teaching (see vv. 16-18).

First of all, Jesus tells us that false prophets are dangerous (wolves). Secondly, they are deceptive (wolves in sheep's clothing). False movements such as the Jehovah's Witnesses come to mind as examples of the wolf masquerading as the lamb. They represent themselves as true children of God—but beware of their sweetness and light! I am not calling for us Christians to hate these *people* for their deception. We should love them for the lost souls that they are—but we should be aware of their subtleties and false claims. We should watch out for their divisive deceptions.

Paul had an experience with "wolves in sheep's clothing" and warned the Ephesian elders: "I know that after I leave, savage wolves will come in among you and will not spare the flock" (Acts 20:29). How right he was! Read Revelation 2:2: "You have tested those who claim to be apostles but are not, and have found them false." After Paul had gone, that magnificent church at Ephesus was torn apart and scattered because of false prophets. John told us how to spot them: "Dear friends, do not believe every spirit, but test the spirits to see whether they are from God, because many false prophets have gone out into the world. This is how you can recognize the Spirit of God: Every spirit that acknowledges that Jesus Christ has come in the flesh is from God" (1 John 4:1-2).

One of the tragedies of our day is the acceptance of the supernatural as always divine by many gullible people—Christians among them. Satan himself is capable of using the supernatural. Indeed, he *is himself* supernatural. We are not to believe every spirit or angel—but we are to put them to the acid test, their attitude toward and treatment of Jesus. Belief is an evidence of spiritual maturity—but so is skepticism! If we do not fall for every "wind of doctrine," we are showing spiritual discernment, the demonstration of our spiritual maturity. The tests revolve around the deity of Christ, his incarnation, and confession of him as Lord and Savior.

We can also check the spirits and cults by their fruit (see Matt. 7:16-20). Their lifestyle won't give them away, for many false prophets might live a more disciplined life than the average Christian. Their zeal and enthusiasm may be greater than the average Christian's, too. We evangelicals, because we rightly believe heaven is a gift and cannot be earned, unfortunately quite often lack zeal and enthusiasm. Not so the cultist who is trying to work his way to heaven. Another indication of false fruit is the error the cultists project, the false teaching they present.

Our Victory

The path of victory lies through the Word of God. Those who are exposed to a balanced exposition of God's Word are equipped to fight the spiritual battle that is raging in our world today. A steady diet of the Word of God is the best battle ration. It provides allround nourishment for the Christian to strengthen him for his task.

I'm not advocating simply a knowledge of the "four spiritual laws" or any other series of proof texts to back up our spiritual convictions. We Christians are called upon to have a balanced view of the Scriptures in their totality.

The people of Laish as described in Judges 18 lost their lives because of carelessness and complacency. But Revelation 2:2-4 shows that, in the midst of vigilance ("deeds, . . . hard works and . . . perseverance"), the church at Ephesus lost their love. John is told to write to them: "Yet I hold this against you: You have forsaken your first love." They had been so careful, so negative, so against everything that they had lost their love. What a tragedy!

The secret of the victorious Christian life lies between careless-ness at the one end and extreme carefulness at the other. The victorious Christian life is a balanced approach. It requires a com-prehensive grasp of the dangers that abound for the Christian and the resources available in Christ. Concentration on the dangers can lead to evangelical paranoia. Indifference to them can lead to spiri-tual disaster. Ignorance of the resources can produce hopelessness and despair, but a healthy understanding of the opposition and a holy dependence on Christ leads to victory.

MAKING IT PRACTICAL

1. What are some of the ways Satan might try to influence or have an effect on a Christian's life? How can we fortify ourselves against his schemes?

2. What do we mean when we talk about "the world" as one of the enemies of the Christian? How does the world tend to influence us and cause us to be less effective?

3. What is our best weapon against our own sinful nature?

4. What are some ways we can tell the false teacher from the true?

5. What is the "best battle ration" for the Christian?

Not everyone who says to me, "Lord, Lord," will enter the kingdom of heaven, but only he who does the will of my Father who is in heaven. Many will say to me on that day, "Lord, Lord, did we not prophesy in your name, and in your name drive out demons and perform many miracles?" Then I will tell them plainly, "I never knew you. Away from me, you evildoers!"

Matthew 7:21-23

19

Obedience

We have reached a portion of the Sermon on the Mount which I consider to be one of the most important in this challenging section of the Scriptures. The crux of this passage is found in verse 21, where Jesus says, "he who does the will of my Father." It is terribly possible for a man to make a great profession, "Lord, Lord," and to be involved in a spiritual ministry like prophecy—without knowing the Lord. It's possible to be a phony! One can serve the Savior without having a valid, viable relationship with him. Does this statement shock you? Let me expand on what I mean.

Obedience gives validity to our profession. Service, no matter how spectacular, is no substitute for obedience. Our modern day is seeing a startling reaction against authority, an intense distaste for obedience. This movement seems to be a natural outgrowth of our democratic philosophy when it gets out of control. Government is to be of the people, for the people, and by the people, according to the democratic principle, and this can be beautiful as long as it is operating ideally. Today, however, we are beginning to see signs of a breakdown in the process. Unfortunately, as I pointed out in a previous chapter, this kind of thinking can result in what the writer of Judges described: "In those days Israel had no king; everyone did as he saw fit" (17:6). The democratic system, out of control, can degenerate into anarchy. The erosion of authority can accompany the democratic process when confidence in government declines, as it has in our day. It's a two-way street. People naturally rebel against authority—and if the authority figure has feet of clay, their declining confidence accelerates that rebellion and disillusionment.

Obedience is lacking on the family level, in the political realm, on the educational scene, even in the sports arena. And in the church we have a similar situation. People in our churches who profess that God is God and Jesus Christ, the risen Lord, is his Son are also reacting against his authority. The situation is so serious that we have people in our churches who do not even know what obedience is! This is the area of the Christian life we are going to examine in this chapter. Without question obedience is the evidence of faith.

The early Christian creed set out for all the world to hear the blessed message that "Jesus Christ is Lord." This was the fundamental credo of the early church, and the lordship of Christ requires the acknowledgment of lordship—obedience. Obedience may not be the most popular of subjects, but if Jesus is to be acknowledged as Lord, obedience is crucial to our understanding of what the Christian life really means.

The Significance of Obedience

Obedience was an integral part of our Lord's lifestyle. It is difficult for the finite human mind to fathom why the one who was coequal with the Father, the One who set forth the world with his hands, should have to be obedient. Jesus spelled it out for all to hear when he said, "For I have come down from heaven not to do my will but to do the will of him who sent me" (John 6:38). Why did Jesus leave heaven's glory for the griminess of earth? Obedience. His Father's will had supremacy in his life.

In Christ's life

Our modern way seems to be, "If I want to, I will. And if I don't want to, I won't!" We seem to have little concept of obedience to a power greater than ours. Humans are self-sufficient and self-satisfied. But a fundamental fact of spiritual experience is this: The servant is no greater than his master. As Christians, we are servants of the Most High God—and what he tells us to do should be our command for life. Without doubt, our Savior's obedience was his *motivation for service.*

Secondly, obedience was his *motivation for suffering:* "Going a little farther, he fell with his face to the ground and prayed, 'My Father, if it is possible, may this cup be taken from me. Yet not as I will, but as you will' " (Matt. 26:39). The scene is the Garden of Gethsemane immediately before the Crucifixion. Jesus knew what he was facing, and he was repelled by it—appalled at the immensity and horror of what faced him on Calvary. But the Lord Jesus learned obedience through the things that he suffered (Heb. 5:8).

Obedience was also his *motivation for sacrifice:* "Your attitude should be the same as that of Christ Jesus: Who, being in very nature God, did not consider equality with God something to be grasped, but made himself nothing, taking the very nature of a servant, being made in the human likeness. And being found in appearance as a man, he humbled himself and became obedient to death—even death on a cross!" (Phil. 2:5-8) Obedience was at the root of our Savior's earthly lifestyle, and he is our example in obedience.

In our lives

We also see significance of obedience in our own spiritual experience. Paul mentions it in Acts 26:19: "So then, King Agrippa, I was not disobedient to the vision from heaven." In the next verse (26:20), Paul clarifies the content of the message he presented in obedience to the heavenly vision: "First to those in Damascus, then to those in Jerusalem and in all Judea, and to the Gentiles also, I preached that they should repent and turn to God and prove their repentance by their deeds."

Repentance is a command—and it is to evidence itself through practical "deeds." Our lifestyle as followers of the Master today should also prove the reality of repentance in our hearts. Have you noticed how repentance is played down in Christian circles today? It seems that all one has to do is "make a decision" and join a flock of followers moving to the front—but genuine conversion demands repentance, a drastic turnaround in one's lifestyle, a radical change of mind.

Repentance is more than a momentary emotional reaction to a powerful gospel message. It is a conscious change of direction, a totally new lifestyle that shows a turnaround. This was what Jesus was referring to when he talked about those who said, "Lord, Lord," but didn't mean it from their hearts. We talk about "backsliders" in the church today, but I sometimes wonder if these people ever had anything to "slide out of"—if they ever came to the Savior in true repentance.

Obedience is also an end product of *regeneration:* "You were dead in your transgressions and sins, in which you used to live when you followed the ways of this world and of the ruler of the kingdom of the air, the spirit who is now at work in those who are disobedient" (Eph. 2:1-2). Paul puts his finger on the source of disobedience—Satan. Peter also dealt with this issue: "Therefore, prepare your minds for action; be self-controlled; . . . As *obedient* children, do not conform to the evil desires you had when you lived in ignorance. But just as he who called you is holy, so be holy in all you do" (1 Pet. 1:13-15, italics mine). These two passages dovetail beautifully and call for a radically new lifestyle no longer following the "ruler of the kingdom of the air" but instead following the Holy One. I am convinced that we cannot follow both routes. If we try to have a form of godliness but deny its power (the Savior's power), we are of our father the devil—not our Savior the Lord. My lifestyle must indelibly show whether I have truly repented and been regenerated by the power of God. If I find obedience to God onerous and the demands of Jesus burdensome, then I had better make sure that I am really in the family of God by repentance and regeneration.

Obedience is also an expression of *relationship*. When someone becomes a Christian, that person enters into a relationship with Jesus Christ as both Lord and Savior. Notice the interesting phrase in Matthew 7:23, "I never knew you." What is Jesus saying? That he had never heard of me? No. He is talking about an intimacy of relationship with the living God—a "knowledge" that will leave an indelible imprint upon my life, a *personal* relationship. How do we know we have that relationship? By the fruit of obedience operating in our lives. How can we talk about lordship if our lives fly in the face of what our Lord demands? Jesus asks in Luke 6:46, "Why do you call me, 'Lord, Lord,' and do not what I say?" What Jesus is stating is this: Don't confess me as Lord unless you are willing to do what I say. The inescapable evidence of relationship is obedience.

What is obedience? It's an expression of a relationship to the Lord, a relationship of love. If I really love the Lord, it is bound to show itself in my actions. If I am not obedient, then I have a right to really question whether I have a relationship to the Lord at all. Paul said this: "For it is by grace you have been saved, through faith—and this not from yourselves, it is the gift of God—not by works, so that no one can boast. For we are God's workmanship, created in Christ Jesus to do good works" (Eph. 2:8-10). We are saved by grace, but the evidence of our salvation, our faith, is found in works—obedience to the Lord's demands and commands. James put it another way: the evidence of faith is works. This is the significance of obedience. We cannot escape it.

Some Substitutes for Obedience

One of the first substitutes that comes to mind is *superficial worship*. The word *Lord* is a simple, one-syllable word. It is so easy to say that even a child can mouth it. The problem is, we can use the word in such a way as to make it devoid of content. Even though we say "Lord, Lord," we can be on the verge of spiritual bankruptcy. A superficial use of the word in a meaningless ritual is just that—meaningless. It is an empty form, without power or content.

Another substitute is *spurious witness*. As we pointed out in the last chapter, it is possible for false prophets to arise in the church, and these are also the ones he does not know. Such people may claim the authority of Jesus and call themselves Christians, but he will have to say, "I never knew you," because they do not have a personal relationship with him. The world around us is full of those who claim to be followers of Christ—but he does not know them. They are spurious witnesses.

Then there is the substitute of *spectacular works*. Without for one moment denying the possibility of God doing spectacular things, always remember that a craving for spectacular events is not necessarily evidence of a life of discipleship.

Some Steps to Obedience

The first step to obedience is a *desire to do God's will*. Where does that come from? It comes from the new nature, the new spirit implanted in us when we turn to the Savior. The old nature pulls us toward disobedience, but the new nature gives us the desire to do the will of our Father in heaven. This doesn't mean I never disobey, or that I am always triumphant, never defeated by the old nature that still lives in me. It merely means that I *desire* to please him, to obey him. If my basic desire is to obey God and do his will, then I am no longer constantly demanding my own way. That is the first step to obedience.

The second step is to *discover God's will*. His will does not come as writing in the sky or necessarily in remarkable experiences. No, the usual way we discover his will is by letting the Word of God permeate us with his message and his promises. The Holy Spirit will inspire us and interpret his will to our own hearts. There is no substitute for the Word of God in this process. This is another important and indispensable step toward obedience and the discovery of the Christ-filled life.

The third step is a deep and ongoing filling or *empowering of the Holy Spirit to do the will of God.* Jesus said, "Now that you know these things, you will be blessed if you do them" (John 13:17). Matthew 7:21 says, "Not everyone who says to me, 'Lord, Lord,' will enter the kingdom of heaven, but only he who *does* the will of my Father who is in heaven" (italics mine). It is relatively easy to be caught up in the spectacular, or simply to become involved in hypocritical action, or to adopt superficial standards. But all these things do not impress our Lord. The true disciple must demonstrate love by obedience, by truly acknowledging the lordship of Christ in every area of life. This is the key area, the pivotal point that reveals our true relationship to Jesus Christ. Anything else is sham and superficiality—empty form, devoid of reality.

MAKING IT PRACTICAL

1. What do you think of the author's statement that we "can serve the Savior without having a valid, viable relationship with him"?

2. "The democratic system, out of control, can degenerate into anarchy." In what ways can you see this happening today?

3. While the world around us responds negatively to most authority, what are some of the repercussions we see daily? What does this tell us about the importance of obedience?

4. If I am not obedient to the Lord, what am I really saying about the place God has in my life, and about my relationship with him?

5. What can we learn about obedience from Christ's example?

6. What are some specific steps we can take to be more like him in our daily decisions and attitudes?

"Therefore everyone who hears these words of mine and puts them into practice is like a wise man who built his house on the rock. The rain came down, the streams rose, and the winds blew and beat against that house; yet it did not fall, because it had its foundation on the rock. But everyone who heard these words of mine and does not put them into practice is like a foolish man who built his house on sand. The rain came down, the streams rose, and the winds blew and beat against that house, and it fell with a great crash."

When Jesus had finished saying these things, the crowds were amazed at his teaching, because he taught as one who had authority, and not as their teachers of the law.

Matthew 7:24-29

20
Wisdom

Jesus knew that only two possible reactions could come from those who heard him—and from us who have been exploring the Sermon on the Mount today. Possibility number one was that those who heard him would do what they heard. Possibility number two was that they would *not* do what they heard. As we look into the Word for ourselves, there are only two possible reactions. We either do what we have heard—or we fail to do what we have heard.

These are the possibilities Jesus gives as he concludes the Sermon on the Mount. Now we must examine our own lives in the light of what he has told us. Will we find ourselves listed among the wise persons who do what Jesus says—or will we be one of the foolish ones who builds his house of life upon the sand? What difference has it made—this exposure to the Sermon on the Mount? Are we going to react like the foolish man—or are we going to show wisdom?

Wisdom Makes People Sensible

The sensible people are those who pay attention to the teachings of Jesus Christ. Many profess to believe the Bible from cover to cover—but they never spend time in it. They lack an appetite for it; they have no concern for what it says. Many make great claims for the infallibility, the inerrancy of the Bible—but they don't seem to follow through with the logical conclusion of such an assertion. They fail to study the Word.

Why is it sensible to pay attention to the teachings of Jesus? Because his teachings always project *authority*. This authority was what aroused his enemies to oppose his teachings. And this same authority should encourage us to follow him faithfully. The wise person knows that Jesus is the only one who can teach with authority (Matt. 7:29). The problem with many Christians is that they do not know what Jesus said because they have not spent time in diligent, purposeful study of his Word. If the church is to produce wise people, they must be people of the Book. This is the only authoritative source of true wisdom.

Christ's teaching also produces *amazement*: "The crowds were amazed at his teaching" (Matt. 7:28). Why isn't there more amazement in Christian circles today? I believe it is because people do not really listen, they do not really *hear* what is being said. A wise person is one who is constantly amazed as he or she pays attention to the teaching of Jesus, because his teaching shows authority.

Christ's teachings should also produce *action*: "Everyone who hears these words of mine and *puts them into practice* . . ." (Matt. 7:24, italics mine). The sensible person acts on Jesus' teaching. The Bible talks about two kinds of wisdom. One is theoretical insight into various areas of knowledge. But Jesus is not calling for that kind of wisdom here in the Sermon on the Mount. The wisdom he is emphasizing is prudence, a practical rather than a theoretical insight. A prudent person can translate theory into practice. The truly wise person can put Jesus' principles into operation.

There are three instances of this kind of wisdom which I would like to point out from the Scriptures. "I am sending you out like sheep among wolves. Therefore be as *shrewd* as snakes and as innocent as doves," Jesus said in Matthew 10:16 (italics mine). Jesus is not telling his disciples here to go out with all the knowledge of the ages in their heads. He is telling them to go out and put into practice what he has taught them, using common sense in the midst of difficult situations.

"Who then is the faithful and *wise* servant, whom the master has put in charge of the servants in his household . . . ?" Jesus asks in Matthew 24:45 (italics mine). Here we see sensible action mixed with truth. Jesus said a wise man is like a servant whose master has gone away, leaving this servant with the responsibility of feeding the people (see v. 46). One way of feeding God's people is by giving them the truth, making absolutely certain they are discovering what they need to know.

One further thought on wisdom: "Five of them (the virgins) were foolish, and five were *wise,*" said Jesus in Matthew 25:2 (italics mine). The truly wise person is prepared for the Lord's return. The wise person will not be caught unprepared, as were the five foolish girls.

The wise person also resists antagonism to Christ's teachings: "Everyone who hears these words of mine and puts them into practice is like a wise man. . . . But everyone who hears . . . and does not put them into practice is like a foolish man," said Jesus in Matthew 7:24 and 26. Notice the antagonism between the two reactions. The person who hears the Word of God and is antagonistic (does not do it) is simply demonstrating his estrangement from God. The wise man, on the other hand, is demonstrating his close relationship to the Savior.

We occasionally hear of Christians who have seemingly lost their interest in serving the Savior. They give the impression that they have done their bit, and that they no longer have anything to offer the church or the world around them. This is an example of the kind of antagonism I am talking about here. Maybe it is not *disinterest* they are showing. *Perhaps it is disbelief.* Nothing will kill a church more effectively than to be full of unbelieving believers. Disobedience, disinterest, and disbelief are symptomatic of hard-hearted antagonism under a cloak of evangelicalism. Such lives are built on sand, not the rock of our salvation.

Wisdom Makes People Secure

The apostle talks about people who are driven about by every wind of doctrine. He tells us there will be some who are led astray by cunning fables. There will also be those who start the race, but never complete it. But the wise person will be not only sensible but secure—with a foundation on the rock.

First of all, note that the man who built his house on a rock had a secure base. "Blessed are you, Simon son of Jonah, for this was not revealed to you by man, but by my Father in heaven. . . . You are Peter, and on this *rock* I will build my church, and the gates of Hades will not overcome it" (Matt. 16:17-18, italics mine). The rock referred to here was not Peter but his classic statement of faith in the previous verse: "You are the Christ." This is the rock of our faith—the blessed person of the Lord Jesus Christ, and the truth of his coming.

There is a movement afoot in the church today which troubles me. It is the emphasis that we should come to Christ for what we can get from him. We are told that he rescues failures, that he makes champions, that he assures business success. This is not Christianity. This is not the rock on which we rest our faith. Jesus is the truth, and I become a secure person when I rest my faith on him. I'm not talking about an emotional high—I'm referring to an objective faith, a secure resting on the foundation of Jesus Christ.

What does it mean to build the house of faith upon the rock? It means that circumstances cannot shake it; the winds of persecution cannot sway it. The emphasis here is not on the house, but on the foundation. The word translated "build" is the same word Paul used in 1 Corinthians 10:23 for the idea of edifying or building up the church: " 'Everything is permissible'—but not everything is constructive." The wise person is also interested in building up the Christian community. This is often overlooked in the church today. We emphasize the vertical relationship (getting right with God) but we miss the horizontal (living in community with other believers). We are in relationship to other Christians—and we have responsibilities to them. The wise person builds people up in terms of

Christian character, Christian community, and Christian concern. Paul tells us, "Therefore encourage one another and build one another up, just as in fact you are doing."

Are many learning the truths of the Scriptures through us? Are we feeding anyone, motivating them by sharing the Word with them? If the answer is yes, we are wise servants, faithful and sensible in our fulfillment of his will. The wise person, the secure person, is an encourager, one who builds others up.

Wisdom Makes People Stable

The Lord Jesus makes it quite clear that winds will come, and rains will descend. They will beat on the house of our lives. When the testing comes, will we be stable enough to survive? What are some of the areas in which we will be tested? What about doctrine? False prophets dressed as sheep who are really wolves can advance upon us. Do we understand the difference between truth and error?

What about the relational life? Jesus said, "Leave your gift there in front of the altar. First go and be reconciled to your brother; then come and offer your gift (Matt. 5:24). Have I done any reconciling lately? How are my relationships with those in my immediate family, those in my extended family, those in the family of God? Have I been making progress in this area? Am I tempted in any relational area? Or tempted by lust? Is this an area where the tempter can attack me?

Jesus also talked about some practical areas of life: "Do not store up for yourselves treasures on earth, where moth and rust destroy, and where thieves break in and steal" (Matt. 6:19). Am I living a disciplined life so far as my finances are concerned? Have I undergone testing and temptation in this area of my life? Am I being sane and sensible in my financial life?

Paul left us a word of warning: "If you think you are standing firm, be careful that you don't fall!" (1 Cor. 10:12). The most sensible, the most secure, the most stable saint can fall flat on his face—but read on: "No temptation has seized you except what is common to man. And God is faithful; he will not let you be tempted beyond what you can bear. But when you are tempted, he will also provide a way out so that you can stand up under it" (1 Cor. 10:13). Notice that the way of escape is not avoidance—but standing up under it. God does not allow the testing to come into your life that you might be able to *avoid* it, but that you might discover how secure, how stable you are in the midst of the testing. He will only allow things to come into your life that you can cope with in the strength that he gives.

Have we heard him speak with authority—and does he have full authority over our lives? This is the key to blessed living. The life of sensibility, security, and stability is built on the rock. How thankful we should be for the firm foundation in the midst of a world that is floundering around us. This is what gives Christians that extra spark, that added impetus, to face our world with strength and stability when all around us is weak and unstable.

Christians are under Christ's authority, and our disciplined lives are to show it. Let's allow the Sermon on the Mount to be lived out in our lives! Where do we get the power and authority, the strength and ability to live up to the standards presented in this Sermon? From the one who preached it himself!

MAKING IT PRACTICAL

1. How do you respond to the author's assertion that people can be divided into the wise and the foolish?

2. How do you react to the words: sensible, secure, and stable?

3. Reread the "wise" passages listed by the author. What did these people have in common?

4. What about the "foolish"? What did they have in common?

5. Have you ever known a person who was considered particularly wise? Describe that person? What made that person wise?

6. In what areas of your life do you lack wisdom? In what areas do you feel wiser?